P9-DBQ-557

THE SPRINGS
OF
CREATIVITY

H. WESTMAN

THE SPRINGS
OF
CREATIVITY

WITH AN INTRODUCTION TO PART THREE

BY SIR HERBERT READ

WILMETTE, ILLINOIS

CHIRON PUBLICATIONS

1986

ST. PHILIP'S COLLEGE LIBRARY

STANDARD BOOK NUMBER: 0-933029-05-5

LIBRARY OF CONGRESS CATALOG CARD NUMBER: 86-70771

CHIRON PUBLICATIONS, 400 LINDEN AVENUE, WILMETTE, ILLINOIS 60091

©1986 BY CHIRON PUBLICATIONS. ALL RIGHTS RESERVED

PUBLISHED 1961. SECOND EDITION 1986

PRINTED IN THE UNITED STATES OF AMERICA

"... that man may come, may come unto the gen'ral dance."

Acknowledgments

I AM INDEBTED to Mr. Leroy Leatherman, the American novelist, without whose selfless efforts this book would not have found its present form. I am grateful to him for his manifold contributions and suggestions, and in particular for his having spent his considerable artistic gifts in the writing of this very complicated material.

I am grateful to the artist for her permission to present her case in this book, thus revealing her innermost creative processes to a wider public in the interest of science and art.

I am indebted to all of my patients, who, through their participation in the psychotherapeutic relationship, enriched my insight, and I am grateful to those who gave me permission to use their dream material in this book.

I am grateful to Dr. H. H. Oldham, C.B.E.; to J. Kendall Wallis, M.D.; and to Mr. Andrew Nelson Lytle, each of whom read the manuscript and offered most helpful criticism. I am grateful to Mr. M. Bergmann for drawing my attention to Ghiberti's "Akedah"; to the trustees of the British Museum, to the Bodleian Library at Oxford, the Victoria and Albert Museum in London, the Museo Nazionale del Bargello in Florence, the Staatsbibliothek in Munich, the Niedersächsische Landesgalerie in Hanover, the Prado in Madrid, and the Bollingen Foundation in New York for their assistance in assembling the illustrations.

All translations from foreign works are my own unless otherwise indicated.

I also thank the following for permission to use various quotations:

George Allen & Unwin Ltd. for two quotations from *Human Knowledge* by Bertrand Russell.

The American-Scandinavian Foundation for a verse from "Hóvamál" in *The Poetic Edda* by Henry Adams Bellows.

vii

Acknowledgments

Bollingen Foundation, Inc. for passages from *Spirit and Nature, Papers from the Eranos Yearbooks,* Bollingen Series XXX.1; *The Practice of Psychotherapy* by C. G. Jung, Bollingen Series XX; and *Philosophies of India* by Heinrich Zimmer, Bollingen Series XXVI.

E. J. Brill Ltd. for a passage from *The Gospel According to Thomas,* edited by A. Guillaumont, Henri-Charles Puech, Gilles Quispel, W. Till, and Y. 'Abd al-Masih, copyright by E. J. Brill Ltd.

The University of Chicago Press for quotations from *The Human Condition* by Hannah Arendt, copyright © 1958 by the University of Chicago; *The Babylonian Genesis* by Alexander Heidel, copyright © 1954 by the University of Chicago; *The Complete Greek Tragedies, Aeschylus I,* "The Eumenides," translated by Richmond Lattimore, copyright © 1957 by the University of Chicago; and *The Protestant Ethic* by Paul Tillich, copyright 1948 by the University of Chicago.

Corpus Scriptorum Christianorum Orientalium for a passage from *Sancti Ephraem Syri in Genesim et in Exodum Commentarii.*

Coward-McCann, Inc. for a passage from *Lord of the Flies* by William Golding, copyright © 1955 by William Golding.

Eugen Diederichs Verlag for two quotations from *Die Edda,* translated by Felix Genzmer.

Encyclopedia Britannica for a passage from the Eleventh Edition.

Harcourt, Brace and Company, Inc. for two passages from *Four Quartets* by T. S. Eliot, copyright 1943 by T. S. Eliot; and for a passage from *Oedipus at Colonos* by Sophocles, An English Version by Robert Fitzgerald, copyright 1941 by Harcourt, Brace and Company, Inc.

Harper & Brothers for a passage from *Historical Geography of the Holy Land* by George Adam Smith.

Harvard University Press for a passage from *Thinking and Experience* by H. H. Price.

The Hogarth Press Ltd. for a quotation from *The Complete Psychological Works of Sigmund Freud,* Standard Edition, Volume XVII.

The Jewish Publication Society of America for quotations from *Legends of the Jews* by Louis Ginzberg.

Jüdischer Verlag for a quotation from Volume VI of *Der Babylonische Talmud. Mit Einschluss der vollständigen Mischna. Vollständige deutsche Uebertragung in 12 Bänden von Lazarus Goldschmidt.* Jüdischer Verlag GmbH, Berlin.

Little, Brown & Company for a passage from the *Agamemnon* by Aeschylus, translated by Edith Hamilton in *Mythology.*

Luzac & Company Ltd. for two passages from *The Epic of Gilgamish,* translated by R. Campbell Thompson.

The Macmillan Company, New York, and Sidgwick & Jackson, Ltd., London, for a passage from *The Wonder that was India* by A. L. Basham.

W. W. Norton & Company, Inc., for a passage from *The Psychiatric Interview* by Harry Stack Sullivan.

Oxford University Press, Inc. for passages from *Natural Science and the Spiritual Life* by John Baille; *Oedipus at Colonos* by Sophocles, translated by Lewis Campbell in *Fifteen Greek Plays;* and *Benedict de Spinoza* by H. F. Hallett.

Pantheon Books Inc., New York, and Faber & Faber, Ltd., London, for a passage from *Philosophic Problems of Nuclear Science* by Werner Heisenberg.

Acknowledgments

Rascher & Cie., AG, and Bollingen Foundation, Inc., for a passage from _Wirklichkeit der Seele_ by C. G. Jung.

Sir Herbert Read for a passage each from three essays having appeared respectively in _Quadrum,_ May, 1956; _Question, a Journal,_ Winter, 1952; and _The Sewanee Review, Autumn,_ 1953.

A Note to the Reader

THE INTRODUCTION and Part One of this book are based in part on addresses delivered to the American Academy of Psychotherapists in New York City, to the Present Question Conference in England, and to the Society of Analytical Psychology in London. Portions of the material in Part Two were presented to the Eranos Congress in Switzerland in 1936. Part Three, the Case of Joan, was presented in a more technical form to the International Congress of Analytical Psychology in Zurich in the summer of 1958.

The Introduction and the three Parts are vitally related. I have tried in the Introduction and Part One to set down what I consider to be the fundamental steps in the development of the psyche, and to relate these considerations to the human condition in the twentieth century. In Part Two, the Book of Genesis is discussed as an astonishingly accurate poetic revelation of the psyche's ontogenesis and as the true spiritual background in Western tradition, which made possible the development of Depth Psychology as a science. The Case of Joan, Part Three, demonstrates the living process by which the psyche pursues its ontogenetic purposes.

The Case of Joan is unique. It reveals not only one significant phase or aspect of psychic development, it shows *pictorially* the whole process by which, out of dire containment in the unconscious, a creative human being has emerged—in this instance, an artist. But the case pertains directly to every individual's experience of himself and of the wellsprings of human creativity, no matter whether that creativity directs itself into art or science or day-to-day living.

Contents

Illustrations

MOST OF THE Biblical illustrations for this book are the work of *Jewish* artists of the medieval period, a fact which may surprise many readers. The little-known but highly significant contribution they have made to Biblical art is admirably discussed by Jacob Leveen in his book *The Hebrew Bible in Art,* the Schweich Lectures of the British Academy, London, published for the Academy by Oxford University Press, 1944.

The Case of Joan

THE SPRINGS
OF
CREATIVITY

Figure 1. Adam and Eve and the Serpent at the Tree of Knowledge of Good and Evil

Introduction

> I do not address myself to nations but only to those few people among whom it is taken for granted that our civilization does not fall from heaven but is, in the end, produced by individuals. If the great cause fails, it is because the individuals fail, because I fail. So I must first put myself right. And as authority has lost its spell, I need for this purpose knowledge and experience of the most intimate and intrinsic foundations of my subjective being, so as to build my base upon the eternal factors of the soul.[1]

DURING the winter and spring of 1958, when I was preparing the report on the case of Joan that ends this book and is, in a sense, the occasion for it, I had among my patients a man of thirty-five who was a business executive, and highly intellectual. When I showed him some of Joan's pictures that I felt were especially powerful, he looked at them carefully but he did not take them in. He gave the kind of mock shudder that shows that power has not been truly felt, but has been examined, gauged in its threat and quickly turned away from. Then he put the pictures aside and started talking about his own concerns. A few days later I handed him the above quotation from an essay by Dr. C. G. Jung. He was a careful reader and before he looked up he must

3

ST. PHILIP'S COLLEGE LIBRARY

have read this short paragraph five or six times—not, I would guess, to understand it but to get his annoyance under control before it turned into downright anger. Then he asked when the statement had been written. In 1933, I told him, and added that it had been ignored; this was a translation I had done for myself, that particular essay never yet having been published in English. And I said I thought this very regrettable. He looked doubtful.

"Maybe now," he said, "you could find a great many more people who take for granted something so obvious as that civilization is produced by individuals." He had managed to curb his annoyance, but then it seemed to turn into a strong, steady current of uneasiness against which he fought with questions:

"What does he mean by the great cause? Civilization? Humanity? The individual?"

"Put myself right? But how, according to what ethical or moral or transcendental yardstick, if authority has lost its spell?

"He answers that by taking me straight back to the temple of the oracle at Delphi: *Know Thyself?*"

He got up from his chair. "Besides, he doesn't sound like a scientist. He sounds more like an artist full of faith. That annoys me."

He left my office and walked home through the park, seeing, he said later, how thoroughly his reactions to what he had read, and his questions, proved him to be a man of his century, how quickly he had spoken out of preconceptions and conditionings of the mind he had not been aware of. He did not like the subjectivity of this supposed scientist. But he liked even less being pitched back, as he put it, into Delphi. Being of his time, he could not help turning the famous injunction into a question. *"Know thyself?"* became a kind of panicky cry, echoing and re-echoing for him in the stillness of what we call existential despair.

But despair and despair's philosophy, if one can keep one's head, offer a good location from which to look at those assumptions, preconceptions and conditionings out of the past that make the present what it is. My patient's automatic assumption was that since modern psychology is generally accepted as a science, the man who is one of its founders must sound like a scientist; he should speak, that is, with the greatest possible objectivity about facts he had discovered by observation and experiment and by deduction made in strict accordance with logical rules. Those facts, even if they appeared at first as rarified as the recent discoveries of physics, should eventually turn out to be as accurately descriptive as the facts of biology, should cope with the dynamics of the psyche as efficiently as medicine copes with disease.

Most of his generation, as well as most of his elders, have shared this assumption; if they hadn't, they would not have been so eager to take the new vocabulary over into daily conversation. *Neurotic, psychotic, schizophrenic, introverted, extroverted, Oedipus complex, inferiority complex*—if psychology were the science it claimed to be, then these words and phrases stood for scientific facts, the quicker to be observed in others than in oneself, but even so a source of security in their very objective factualness.

The assumption conceals a hope: that the human psyche, the inner world we have been struggling with since the instant we changed from brute to man, might now turn out to be as observable, predictable, controllable and curable as the flesh we inhabit. Both the assumption and the hope conceal an inheritance from the age of rationalism, and they extend in their implications much further than psychology or science itself. They come to a focus in an image of man that accounts for the distresses of this century: "I think, therefore I am."

Descartes's formula to prove his existence is meaningful far beyond philosophy. More than it describes what had been achieved by the uses of human reason, it reveals what had been lost. Before Descartes and before the Reformation, which gave him and all other thinkers the freedom to think, the question had not been *whether* a man existed distinct in his being, but who in his evident existence and individuality he truly was. The Judaeo-Christian tradition had settled that question to the satisfaction of the vast majority of Western men, to the extent that it could be settled before the scientific age began. It is a fascinating paradox that modern science might not exist at all if the Judaeo-Christian insight had been lacking. Professor John Baillie says:

> It is quite clear to me, then, that modern science could not have come into being until the ancient pagan conception of the natural world had given place to the Christian. . . . [The world process] would follow, they

5

all believed, a cyclical course, and some of them even thought they knew the length of time that each cycle would take to accomplish itself. The spectacle of nature was like a continuous performance at a cinema show. Within so many thousand years from now everything in nature would again be exactly as it is today, and so on, times without number, to all eternity. Nor was this merely because the same or similar things would periodically recur within the stream of time, but because, as Aristotle expressly says, the movement of time is itself circular. What Christianity did was, as it were, to roll the circle of time out flat. The rectilinear conception of time, which we all now take for granted, was introduced into Western thought by Christianity.[2]

In reference to the psyche, it is more exact to say that with the development of the Judaeo-Christian tradition the circle, coming round, no longer closed back upon itself but lifted and, coming round, lifted again in a kind of spiraling creativity that had as its source the ineffable unity of God, man and the universe. With the monotheism of the Old Testament, all creation had been discovered to be the work of one God, who was not only creator but lawgiver to His creation. The world was whole, and man was whole within it because he believed himself to be made in the image of the one God. This conviction gave him a relation to the natural order he had never experienced before. Then the Christian mystery of God becoming man gave him the possibility of a new relation to himself. If he had been the prey and victim of the forces of the natural world, he had been equally the prey and victim of the forces of his own nature, that portion of himself that by virtue of its seeming autonomy made him the brother of beasts. But now within the inner world the seemingly unbreakable circle, the pagan's eternal round, irrevocable in its turning back upon itself, was broken and the upward surge of creativity was discovered not only in the natural world but in man himself. He could be related with, no longer subject to, the forces of his own nature. In depending upon the unity of God, man and the universe, this surge depended perforce on the whole of a man, on flesh and spirit, on a potential unity that reconciled the dualities within him.

This was the way the Church—not as an institution but as a dynamic symbolic order, an all-encompassing effort of the human psyche to express in symbolism and to realize in immediate daily life the discoveries it had made—answered the question of who a man truly is. The image of the whole man—as much prone to the dark as to the light, to the irrational as to the rational; as much prone to dreams and visions and the making of symbols and images as to the search for scientific facts—the image of the whole man who by the very fact of his wholeness had a place at the center of things was what, by the time of Descartes, had been lost. One representation of this concept of wholeness appears in the Heiningen Carpet (Figures 2 and 2A).* It was replaced by the image of the rational man who by the use of his rational faculties, with no recourse to those other faculties that had brought him where he was, and by the power of dispassionate observation and objective thought, would be so perfectly related to the physical universe that he might eventually discover its final secret.

It is obvious what this later ideal image of who man is omits, denies as valid experience, rejects as specifically human. Nevertheless this image stands as the point of emergence of a line that comes straight down past Descartes to the eighteenth century and Laplace—for whom, since the universe was a machine and science could explain it, God was a hypothesis man no longer needed—and from him to Darwin in the nineteenth century,[3] and from Darwin to all the logical positivists of our time, who consider man's high-

* The design of the Heiningen Carpet, woven in 1516, is a secular representation of the mediaeval ideal of wholeness. *Philosophia* is placed at the center of things, surrounded circle by circle with satellites who represent man's mental and moral qualities and his achievements in learning. The inner circle holds *Teorica* (speculative knowledge of the truth), *Mechanica* (knowledge and government of actuality), *Physica* (speculative knowledge of Nature), *Practica* and *Logica.* Each, being so placed, is immediately held up to view in its *relative* importance to the center. *Philosophia's* banner bears the legend: "The knowledge of the divine springs from supernatural grace." Since the age of reason, when man lost his sense of the relative importance of his various gifts, qualities and achievements, the *partial* man has sat in *Philosophia's* place and all she represents of love and of human intuition of the Unknown has been shifted to the far periphery. (Reproduced by courtesy of the Victoria and Albert Museum.)

7

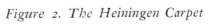
Figure 2. The Heiningen Carpet

Figure 2a. Detail of the Heiningen Carpet, inner circle

est function to be the grinding of general laws out of large collections of "facts." And the line goes straight from them to my young patient who, being typical of his time, has it in his blood, so to speak, to trust nothing but the rational, observable and provable, and to be brought close to anger if, for example, a psychologist allows himself to mention such things as "the eternal factors of the soul."

There is nothing new about pointing to the ideal of the rational man as the source of much of our distress. Our most serious artists and our deepest thinkers in the fields of theoretical science, philosophy and aesthetics have been saying it for a long time. Fortunately our scientists through their own discoveries are now able to see the partiality and onesidedness of absolute faith in the observable fact and are abandoning it as a tenable, workable ideal.* They have realized that the scientist as *observer-pre-*

* "... complete objectivity as usually attributed to the exact sciences is a delusion and is, in fact, a false ideal."—M. Polanyi, *Personal Knowledge* (Chicago, University of Chicago Press, 1958), p. 18.

"... the science of microphysics ... on account of the basic 'complementarity' situation, is faced with the impossibility of eliminating the effects of the observer by determinable correctives, and has therefore to abandon in principle any objective understanding of physical phenomena. . . ."—W. Pauli, quoted by C. G. Jung in "The Spirit of Psychology," in Joseph Campbell, ed., *Papers from the Eranos Yearbook,* Bollingen Series XXX, 1 (New York, Pantheon Books, Inc., 1954), p. 439.

"... while mental events and their qualities can be known without inference, physical events are known only as regards their space-time structure. The qualities that compose such events are unknown—so completely unknown that we cannot say either that they are, or that they are not, different from the qualities that we know as belonging to mental events."—Bertrand Russell, *Human Knowledge* (London, Allen and Unwin, 1951), p. 247.

"... the changes introduced by quantum theory have affected the position of theories of perception in such a way that those aspects of reality characterized by the words 'consciousness' and 'spirit' can be related in a new way to the scientific conception of our time. Classical physics was built on the firm foundation of the recognition of the objective reality of events in time and space which take place according to

dictor, capable of handling his intellect as an instrument detached from all else that makes him a man, is a logical impossibility; that as a man he is inescapably involved in the processes of experiment and is therefore inescapably an *observer-participant.* This means that the scientist (and by implication, man himself) is restored to that humble yet central position in which he is not a godlike spectator and manipulator of a mechanistic universe, but a participant in what is a substantial and abiding mystery.

There was a subtle but critical alienation from the natural order, born of the ideal of objectivity toward it; now, as the scien-

---

natural laws independent of mental activity. This means, of course, that they, in their turn, apply only to such 'objective' processes. Mental processes appear to be only an image of this objective reality which is separated from the world of time-space relations by an unbridgeable gap. Improved modern technique of observation and the enrichment of positive knowledge resulting from it has finally forced us to revise the fundamentals of science and has convinced us that there can be no such firm foundation of *all* perception. . . .

". . . There exist apart from the phenomena of life, still other aspects of reality, i.e., consciousness and, finally, mental processes. We cannot expect that there should be a direct link between our understanding of the movement of bodies in time and space, and of the processes of the mind, since we have learnt from science that *our mental approach to reality takes place, at first, on separate levels which link up, so to speak, only behind the phenomena in an abstract space.* We are now more conscious that there is no definite initial point of view from which radiate routes into all fields of the perceptible, but that *all perception must, so to speak, be suspended over an unfathomable depth.* When we talk about reality, we never start at the beginning and we use concepts which become more accurately defined only by their application. Even the most concise systems of concepts satisfying all demands of logical and mathematical precision can only be tentative efforts of finding our way in limited fields of reality. . . . We are no longer in the happy position of Kepler, who saw the interrelations of the world as a whole as the will of its creator, and who believed himself, with his knowledge of the harmonies of the spheres, to be on the threshold of understanding the Plan of Creation. *But the hope for a great interconnected whole which we can penetrate further and further remains the driving force of research for us too.* [My italics.]"—Werner Heisenberg, *Philosophic Problems of Nuclear Science* (New York, Pantheon Books, Inc., 1952), p. 92.

12

tists agree on this new and fundamental insight, this alienation may grow less. But there has been a much more critical alienation from ourselves and from those other aspects of reality the age of reason omitted, rejected and denied in its conception of who a man truly is and may be; and it is here, in spite of all that the most serious men of our time have said against the rational ideal, that the majority of us have failed to pay attention. It was here, in this area of alienation, that my patient's despair led him to look and to question.

He realized, he said, how difficult it was for him to conceive of harmony among all the various attributes that make men human. His view of things was founded, though he had never thought of it, upon the division of being that was implied by Descartes's proof. Thinking might prove that he existed, but *feeling* could never prove it for him. Any intuition of the unknown was wholly suspect. He realized that he was iconoclastic, innately so. It was not only that the symbol and the poetic image were valueless to him when compared with the scientific fact; he went much further and doubted the gift and the power that bring them into being. He found no security, he said, except in conformity, in the partial view, the rigid opinion and the leap to extremes. But this was true, it seemed to him, of everyone he knew. Wasn't it simply human nature?

It would seem to be, but I believe it is the opposite of man's *true* nature. I believe a man is potentially whole within himself, a unity and totality, and if he can be said really to have a destiny, it lies here, in the realization of this potential wholeness. The psyche is determined by it, for this is the psyche's evolutionary aim and the purpose of its growth.

From the instant in the history of the species when man first glimpsed his possible humanity, from that moment in our own individual histories when we first glimpse it for ourselves, the struggle has been and always is to emerge from the autonomy of nature, to achieve a relationship with the forces of the natural order, *both inner and outer,* so that we are no longer driven blindly by them as primitive man is driven, no longer contained within nature as he is, but *distinct* within it, having as men the power to choose. The psyche has grown and will continue to grow to the degree that this struggle is won or lost.

What emerges in the struggle is human personality. Everything depends upon it. The human condition has always been and will always be directly the product of personality, that indefinable *means* by which a man is related with the world within himself and the world around him. The stage of development of personality, in this sense of the word, and the status man accords to it determine his failures and successes in the cause of humanity, the quality of his social organizations and of his cultural achievements.

We know that man suffers when he is at the mercy of his environment, when he fails to be adequately related to it. We seem to have come close to forgetting that he suffers also from his fellow men when he is regarded as less than a man—used, for example, as a means to an end—and when they fail him and he in turn them in those relationships we call friendship and love. But we have forgotten that he suffers, and suffers most, when he fails in his relation with his own inner world and is at the mercy of himself. Yet it is ultimately upon this latter relation that his individuality, his status as a man and his destiny depend.

The Christian image of the whole man—born out of the conviction that harmony is possible between all the attributes that make a man human, between man and his fellow men, between man and the universe and between man and his God—fostered personality, and while that image was still dominant, life seemed to have much of the richness that comes with the double gaze, the passionate look not only outward upon the wonderful orders of the universe but simultaneously inward upon the equally wonderful and equivalent orders of the psyche. Surely the Middle Ages were far from idyllic, but even so it seems to have been the time when Western man came as close as he has ever come to a condition in which he could bring the full measure of his gifts to bear upon the instant. The Reformation, we know, changed that condition for better and for worse. As a revolt against religious authoritarianism, against incipient idolatry and an extreme of fanciful indulgence that burdened every event in the natural world with "inner" or "religious" meaning, it was necessary. But obviously it went to its own extremes and gave us not only intellectual freedom but also the iconoclasm that has characterized the times ever since.*

Barring hurricanes, earthquakes and the like, we have through our science achieved an amazing relation with the forces of the universe. They almost seem now to be ours to control. But because in our iconoclasm and in our idolatry of the rational man we have ignored other essential aspects of reality, because we have neglected our other gifts and failed to respect those faculties by which we experience the inner world, make use of its potential and communicate its values, we fail in any relation with the forces of the psyche. We fail in personality, in its development and (all our lip service and hypocrisy to the contrary) in the honor we give it.

Iconoclasm intends to destroy the symbol and the image, but it cannot destroy the power inherent in them or the power that brings them into being; "destruction" merely deflects these powers into other channels. Reason may deny the irrational but the irrational remains; light dispels darkness only as far as it can reach. The psyche, like the universe, goes its own way, as it has inevitably done. Its vast energies, which might have been at the service of humanity, now wield something like absolute power over us. The more we have neglected them, the more autonomous they have become; and now we despair in the midst of our comforts and scarcely remember the meaning of friendship and love. We had hoped never again to be surprised by our own brutality and never again to be overwhelmed and swept away by the irrational and uncivilized within us. But no matter how much we hoped, our

---

* "C. G. Jung has called the history of Protestantism a history of continuous 'iconoclasm' ('the destruction of pictures,' i.e., of religious symbols) and, consequently, the separation of our consciousness from the universally human 'archetypes' that are present in the subconscious of everybody. He is right. Protestants often confuse essential symbols with accidental signs. They often are unaware of the numinous power inherent in genuine symbols, words, acts, persons, things. They have replaced the great wealth of symbols appearing in the Christian tradition by rational concepts, moral laws, and subjective emotions. This also was a consequence of the Protestant protest against the superstitious use of the traditional symbols in Roman Catholicism and in all paganism. But here also the protest has endangered its own basis."— Paul V. Tillich, *The Protestant Era* (The University of Chicago Press, Phoenix Books, 1958), p. xix.

experience has been the opposite: we have found ourselves to be masterly in the ways of brutality and destruction.

Instead of standing with high and justifiable pride in the magnificence of our science, we huddle, crowded together, between the disaster just accomplished and the greater and more complete one about to come. In this, we are as primitive as any tribe that ever walked the earth. As surely as primitive man feels himself to be, and is, at the mercy of nature, both inner and outer, we feel ourselves to be at the mercy of our own inventions and social organizations and of still darker forces equally if not more powerful than any we imagine we control by science. We think we have no choice and that therefore we have no responsibility. But the bomb hovering, about to drop, is an exact objective correlative of a portion of our own deepest nature, and it is there so ominously and so obviously because we have chosen not to look and not to listen to the irrational and illogical, the numinous and the dark—those daily experiences. We had hoped to make them reasonable, to conquer them with words;* failing that, we have thought we could turn our backs. But the forces of the psyche never cease to act, and we cannot avoid responding to them. The question is always how, consciously or unconsciously, we do respond. For the psyche, as it pursues its aim, whole means literally *whole* (the etymology of *whole* is very meaningful: it has the same root as *hale,* meaning healthy, and as *holy*). If the individual accepts, as we have done, a partial ideal of what he is and might be, then the urge inherent

* ". . . If rainbows, reflections, mirages and the like had been less common than they are, philosophers would have denied their existence on *a priori* grounds. For how can there be entities which are at once physical and non-physical, in the physical world and yet not of it, existing from some points of view in physical space but not from others, spatial but lacking backs or insides? The fate of mental images, in these latter Verbalistic days, has been somewhat similar. We have the misfortune to live in the most word-ridden civilization in history where thousands and tens of thousands spend their entire working lives in nothing but the manipulation of words. The whole of our higher education is directed to the encouragement of verbal thinking. . . . Let us hope that our successors will be wiser, and will encourage both." H. H. Price, *Thinking and Experience* (Cambridge, Mass., Harvard University Press, 1953), p. 252.

in him to realize and make actual his potential wholeness will be, and is now increasingly, deflected outward, projected onto others or onto a "group" or his society, and eventually varieties of totalitarianism are the result. The more we have failed in *personality,* in any relation with the forces of our being, the farther we have retreated from them into conformity and specialization and into social organizations that promise greater and greater degrees of security the more totalitarian they become—security, that is, from ourselves, of course, from our own human nature.

There is some sense in the retreat. The autonomy of the forces within us is evidently easier to bear if we project it outward into the light of day and suffer and complain about it as the autonomy of the state. But there is a deeper level: as human beings, we must and will have a symbolic order, no matter how partial or finite it may be, or how hedged in and blind to what surrounds it; and whether we know it or not, we require that it be a symbolic order that promises to deal with the *whole* of our experience and with all our needs. We deny the individual in modern society, force him into a common mold and see to it that he conforms. We value him for his function and his uses, never asking *who* he *is* but *what* he *does,* and commit ourselves directly to the impersonality of modern life, to our failure in human relations and to the falsification of our individual and collective responsibilities. But all the time we retain our sense of individuality and of the unique man. The proof of it is everywhere, but displayed with tragic distortion in the gigantic portraits we set up of *Führers,* commissars, political candidates, religious revivalists, film stars. We continue to create symbols and images, but we conceive them as the trappings of social and political groups. The portraits, the hammers and sickles and swastikas, have an amazing power over modern man for no reason other than that they are projections of his own needs as a man. They prove the extent to which his very perception of those needs is faulty and the extent to which his nature itself is debased.

We continue to demand ritual and get it as pathetic (comic, if Aristophanes were here) travesty in the new social and political rites.

"And never mind what some moralists say, customs and rites live among the people." This statement was addressed recently to *Izvestia* by a Soviet automobile-factory foreman named Usakovsky. He wrote to point out the need for these in his society, arguing that his people were married in churches and had their children baptized, not from any belief in God, but because they like "solemn and picturesque ritual." *Izvestia* is, as a result, sponsoring a contest, offering prizes, in a search for "Soviet rites."[4] The East German Government already has such a system of rites to care for its citizens from birth to death; the officiates are trained party members.

In this way, not only in overtly totalitarian societies but, in various ways, in "free" societies as well we shape the symbolic order toward completeness and sufficiency.

All of this is a predictable sequence of events. Given the original, fatal confusion about man's nature, the failure in personality and the consequent projection outward of what is deepest in us, it is certain that the individual will come to find his identity in the object of that projection and will eventually look to it in expectation of being put right, not only with the world and with his fellow men, but also with himself. When this happens, the object of the projection, whether it is another individual or a "group" (anything from the street gang to the state), becomes the arbiter of moral and ethical values, the source of "rightness." The circle turns back upon itself; the pagan's Eternal Round is re-established; choice and individual responsibility vanish from the scene of action.

The modern man, for whom traditional authorities (king, state, church, family) have lost their spell and for whom no such artifice as a "group" is adequate, finds himself, like my patient, without any moral, ethical or transcendental yardstick by which to decide what "rightness" might conceivably be. He is driven back upon himself and finds there what he calls "emptiness" but what is really a lack of any relation with the forces of his own inner world, and is thus in utter subjection to them. So he sinks into despair, if not into moral stupor. All of this is evidence of our present condition, reflections in a crazy mirror of who a man is and may be, of the ultimate sources of his motives and his actions and of what is inherent in him as a human being.

My patient went back often to Dr. Jung's statement and to the questions he had raised against it, and once he asked if he might take another look at Joan's drawings. This time he seemed to study them carefully, but when he gave them back he said, "I do not see what this kind of art has to do with civilization, let alone with me."

I said I thought it had a great deal to do with civilization because through her work Joan had looked directly, though certainly not *consciously,* into the inner world, had looked straight at those forces of her nature that had come within a hairsbreadth of destroying her as a person. She had gained thereby a degree of relationship with those forces, and so to some extent could now choose for herself, and thus had to some extent put herself *right.* If more of us had been willing and able to do this, we would be less primitive, less afraid, more responsible and more human, and our civilization would be more worthy of the name.

"But doesn't this lead us," he asked, "into a very strange country?"

It does if one has, as he did, the doubts typical of our time. He came finally to admit he doubted, as so many do, that art or religion had much in the long run to do either with him or with civilization. Wouldn't values, rightness, eventually be found to spring entirely from the practical and reasonable? Wasn't the science of psychology discovering new things every day about why we do what we do? Wasn't it making the so-called irrational rational, understandable, avoidable? If it wasn't, then why was he sitting there opposite me?

Science, and psychology *as a science* is concerned with facts, not values. It analyzes the past, the world that has become fact, and on the basis of its findings predicts within limits a likely future; but it cannot and does not pretend to say whether it is good or bad that past, present or future are what they may be, and it cannot and does not aspire to justify the uses we make of the powers with which it supplies us. It may give us facts on whose basis our choices may be made more easily and safely, but that is all. J. H. Oldham wrote:

> ". . . our choice of action, whilst pertaining to the facts, is in the main an adventurous committal to an unknown and unforeseeable future."[5]

Again, this leads into strange country, but only if, like my patient, you doubt that there may be kinds of discovery other than the scientific. The *discoveries* revealed by the work of art, by symbols and images; the *discoveries* of our dreams, the insights into the inner world these things constitute: it was impossible for him to take these as such, as valid and meaningful to humanity in the way that scientific discovery obviously is. He could take it quickly for granted that civilization does not drop from heaven but is produced by individuals, and that logically, the rightness or wrongness of a civilization would depend upon the individual, his actions and his responsibility for them. But meaningful action, the only sort that could conceivably produce and sustain civilization, implies moral and ethical values, and these are matters of the soul. No matter how closely our choices and our actions square with the facts of our social existence and our situation in the outer world, they fail in value if they do not also square with the facts of the inner world. It is the individual who discovers by his "adventurous committal" the nature of that world and so discovers the truly moral and ethical, the truly good and meaningful, and their opposites. He does it and is able to do it only to the degree that he has achieved *personality*—only to the degree, in other words, that he is himself and knows himself, knows he is not his past nor his environment nor his society nor his fellow men, knows he is *sustained of course by all these things* but is identified with none of them.

To all this my patient, being not only very much a man of his time but being also very human, objected vigorously. To tell a man that the success or the failure of the great cause is in his hands may not upset him too much. Tell him, however, that as an individual he bears the burden of discovery of the ultimate values by which he and his fellow men are to succeed or fail, and you may send him, past vigorous objection, to despair. For to tell him this places responsibility squarely where it belongs, and the burden is very great. It is much easier to let our choices and our actions remain unintentional, directed by some other authority than ourselves.

> For the good I would I do not,
> but the evil which I would not, that I do.

St. Paul, with his great insight, set down perfectly in these two lines the plight of men when they fail in personality. Choice, the human prerogative and distinction, becomes impossible.

My patient chose at last to go back to the subject of the *great cause*. What was it? I said that in my view it is the cause of the whole man, rather than of the partial and functional man; the cause of man in the free exercise of all his gifts and faculties, not a single one of which is inimical to the rest; the cause, therefore, of the psyche itself, in its urge to realize its potential wholeness. To take up this cause necessarily means to attend to the Delphic injunction: "Know Thyself."

"But *what*," he demanded, "does that mean?

"*Who* is the knower?

"*What* is to be known?

"And even if I finally do know it, does that mean I will be more peaceful, more creative?"

So he came to the heart of the matter.

PART ONE

Know Thyself?

"BEFORE Heaven and Earth existed," according to Lao-tzu, "there was something nebulous: silent, isolated, standing alone, changing not, eternally revolving without fail, worthy to be the Mother of all things . . ."[6]

When the God of the Old Testament began His creation, the earth was a desolate waste, with darkness covering the abyss, and He said, "Let there be light" and made the firmament and divided the waters.

There are as many myths about the creation of the cosmos as there are peoples. Science has shown these myths of the origins of the material world to be at best charmingly naive, yet they keep their beauty and power. This is not only because of the grandeur of their language; they are all, I believe. variations on a single, much deeper theme: The creation of the cosmos and the drama of its slow unfolding is a symbol of the poet's experience of his own inner creation and his own slow opening to the light. On their deepest level all these myths are really concerned with the ontogenesis of the psyche itself.

For us, taking our first breaths, there must have been nothing at all but something nebulous; the light, consciousness itself, must have been a long time coming into the waste of darkness, and the waters very slow to divide. That first sense of security that came with the first satisfaction of our creaturely needs must have seemed like the first firm inches of dry land uncovered by the ebb of the primal sea.

Isolated from the start, standing alone, changing not, yet eternally revolving without fail, worthy to be the Mother of all things: this nebulous First Principle Lao-tzu could not name, but described as *Tao*. As First Principle of All Creation, it is never to be named. But if we take the whole statement as an image sprung from the depths of the poet's being, the *inner* cosmos, it seems perfectly to describe the first state and potential of the human psyche at whose center—before anything else, nebulous, something in the midst of seeming nothingness—the poet himself stood in his *intrinsic individuality*. All of our personal stories end up being about what happens to this intrinsic individuality as it shapes itself out of its own unique determination and as it is shaped by events in the inner world and in the world outside.

In the foregoing Introduction I have spoken about human personality as a means of relations with experience, both inner and outer, without which man is no more than biologically human. Man begins, as man, with an intrinsic individuality; it is the human distinction and it is what makes personality possible. Yet personality as a phenomenon, a flowering of the psyche in its development, is, in terms of human history, a relatively recent achievement. Our remote ancestors, and aboriginal peoples in general, cannot be said to have had personality in this sense. They lived in a *participation mystique* with both worlds of experience, having no sense of separateness or distinction from them nor, in fact, any sense that there might be distinctions between them. Their individuality remained nebulous. The events of the natural world and the events of the psyche were matters of force: nature ruled beyond any questioning. As a people, they might master their environment in that they come to terms with it and survive, but the mastery and the survival have a precise limit at the edge of the environment itself. Over the edge, the secure, established relations necessarily collapsed. Their identity resided exclusively in their surroundings and in their participation with them, and this seems to have been the state of things for a very long time. But then individuality asserted itself; the first dim sense of separateness and distinction had come, and with it the primary faculties of the psyche came into play: reflection and—unique to man—the gift of symbolization and imaging.

The creation of the symbol (Greek *syn* "together," *ballein* "to throw") is in itself an affirmation of a state of relationship. Among the ancient Greeks the initiate to the Mysteries was given a fragment of bone, called a *symbola,* which served thereafter to identify him; only when he could show it and prove it to fit its counterpart held by the priest was he admitted to the sanctuary. So the symbol is that which establishes and affirms a relation between the known and the unknown—a most necessary function, since the two *are* vitally related, belong essentially together and may be experienced to correspond. Symbolization, according to A. D. Ritchie, is "the essential act of thought."[7] Certainly it was and is among humanity's first acts of independent thought. Through it early man made his first attempts to experience a human relation with the natural order; his distinction within that order began to dawn upon him. As soon as he was able to see the world of nature as something other than himself, he began to be able to differentiate himself from it; personality became possible as soon as the intrinsic individuality that is his distinction began to be felt.

Each of us experiences very much the same prototypical pattern of development in infancy and early childhood. Each of us begins wholly contained within nature, rather like a fish in the great waters of the world; but by virtue of the psyche's evolution we emerge rapidly and our first gifts come quickly into play.

We seem to begin to be ourselves very early in our lives. In spite of predictable patterns of behavior we all seem to follow, there are subtle variations in our modes of action and reaction, which can only be accounted for by the presence of that something "nebulous" that keeps us unique throughout our lives. Poetically speaking, these modes of action and reaction when working in harmony and balance seem perfectly to correspond to those observable modes of action and reaction by which the natural world appears to be sustained. The modern physicist's picture of "matter" as an aggregation of events held together by a system of forces between them is useful here. The psyche is from the beginning a complex of energies and inertias (as such, an aggregation of events) held together, related, by the tensions between them. It is in the midst of this *primal relation* that our intrinsic individuality

25

is situated. The happenings of pleasure and pain, of needs and their satisfaction or frustration, of the freedom to release our energies or the prevention from doing so, reassure us in that delicate situation or threaten us in it.

The waters of the inner world recede and more land lies dry and open, and it is in our nature to go forth and explore it; but it is equally in our nature to lie still, inert. The inner world, like the outer, is a world of opposites in constant interplay, and we grow in the midst of the tensions between them. It is out of our experience of these events, as we act and react out of our intrinsic individuality, that we begin to have a sense of identity.

The first sense of *who* one is, is naturally founded in one's relations with those aspects of the immediate scene that have satisfied and given pleasure, have not satisfied and given displeasure, have seemed harmonious or not. There is no way of calculating these relations—what pleases one child may drive another into a tantrum. Once past early infancy, our identity lies with the people who are close to us, who seem to know well enough who we are though we ourselves do not. This is a crucial point. When *their* sense of our identity—as their flesh and blood, heirs to their past and heritage and their relations with themselves, with each other and with their world—comes into opposition with our own growing sense of an identity somehow independent of them and all they represent, the struggles begin. But full as the world may be of warring opposites, for the very young child the family is, ideally speaking, where opposites are reconciled. If as a family it is relatively harmonious, the child does not exist nor does he wish to exist separate from it. Whatever forays he makes toward the unknown, he makes out of the security or insecurity of the family; he takes it with him, so to speak, since he does not view himself as in any way distinct from it. This is, in elementary terms, what modern psychology refers to as "identification." It seems to be a primary and natural way the psyche acts in its ontogenesis.

Identification and Anxiety

FOR THE majority of us it seems to be necessary that we progress through a long series of *identifications* before we discover our independence, if we ever do. The *if* is big: Identification as a natural mode of action of the psyche is a part of growth; but it is also, paradoxically, the way back into the psyche's primal inertia. The child progresses through a series of scenes, in each one of which the question of his identity must be settled. Once it is, he tends to stick with that settlement and that scene, for he is known there in the midst of it, thus knows himself and seems secure. He may come, with maturity, to a sense of himself independent of all those people and scenes which once contained him, but he very well may not. We know, for example, that whole societies have been built and have for a time survived in a state of identification with the family and ancestral images. Ancestor worship is very old, but we may often find in the midst of it an opposite, compensatory vision, a nirvana, an ideal ultimate state of utter release from all human connections and relations.

Identification can have dire consequences: ". . . The fathers have eaten a sour grape, and the children's teeth are set on edge."[8] It is not simply a matter of taking on the color and shape, the outward seeming, of the scene and the people within. If the child's identity resides in that scene, with those people, then it truly resides there, functions there, and there is scarcely any question of participation elsewhere. The child's intrinsic individuality leads him to be selective in his identifications; he chooses, unconsciously, what seems to suit him and rejects what does not; but in the very choosing he may take upon himself parental riddles and parental tensions that have nothing at all to do with him *as an individual*. It will then come down to this (and more often than not it does): he will not only be an extension in the natural world of his parents' bodies; he will *also* to an amazing degree be an extension of their psyches—graced perhaps by their graces but doomed, if he is not careful, by their doom, trapped by the necessity to resolve what

27

they failed to resolve, his teeth on edge from all the sour grapes of the past.

Through our identifications we begin to be able at any given moment to sum ourselves up. We come to have an image of ourselves—a composite image, based on the past but framed by the present—by what at the moment identifies us. Owing to the psyche's natural inertia, we tend to keep a firm grip on these momentary summations. Backed as firmly as a picture in a frame by family or school, friends, function or position, we keep our eyes shut to the fact that all lies open above, below and around us. We may go on this way long after the specific identifying scene has been left behind.

If we looked, we should see that the inner world (the real world of our identity) is quite like the world outside, full of the same expanses, full of unexplored ground and bottomless depths. We should eventually see that these two seemingly diverse realities are engaged in constant interplay, and that the problem for us is to proceed with our summations of ourselves until they are no longer momentary, restricted neither by the past nor time nor space, fixed only in that they are the focus of the interplay itself.

The way we experience this interplay—the flux, the warring of opposites—is determined to a great extent by another of the psyche's natural modes of action: *anxiety*. As our vital energies, through our identifications, attach themselves to what is known and seemingly secure, they tend to fall into something like sleep. If we were not naturally anxious, one stage of identification would not give way to another; and if we did not go on being anxious, we should never grow. Anxiety is, therefore, vital to our development. The breadth, scope and richness of personality depend greatly on our experience of anxiety and on how we tolerate its pressures, for it is not only a spur to growth; it is also the psyche's natural way of defending us, as individuals, against the impacts of experience. Defenses are necessary; one could not survive without them. Anxiety builds walls around our intrinsic individuality and holds them as if they were fortresses until it is safe to abandon them and leave them to crumble. So, contrary to popular notions, anxiety is not merely negative. It may lead to despair, but that state is not necessarily bad, either. Though we most often cry out about it in terms of the world's and life's meaninglessness, despair often indicates that our peripheral identifications have failed us and that, past the old walled defenses, the field lies open to the unknown.

In none of these ways do we act by thought or plan, yet we know the qualities of the effects of such actions. When things outside get to be more than we feel we can take, we lose ourselves in fantasy. When we are depressed, threatened within ourselves by something we cannot name, we turn against the outside world, finding the time, not ourselves, out of joint. It is as if by this kind of displacement and projection of the one world upon the other, the tension of the conflict could be reduced. It is not, of course: the conflict remains as violent, the tensions between the opposed forces just as great; but our defenses muffle the uproar.

The Mask and the Shadow

THE GREEK actor's mask was referred to as *persona;* it told the audience what role was being played. The concept of persona in analytical psychology is much the same. In the world of action, everyone has roles to play with those he loves, works with, casually meets, casually passes by; a part is to be acted in all these meetings and confrontations, and much of its style is dictated by one's estimate of the scene, of one's situation within it, and of the people and what they might expect, demand or require. The persona is the total impression we mean to give in the specific situation, to the extent that we can control it; it is a product of our experience and of our response to that experience, a subtle molding by the psyche of a mask for the world to see. The finished product (and it is often finished and set hard early in our lives) is the face that in our partial awareness we have found to work best. It is not a "false" face, but rather a natural offensive-defensive covering. It only becomes false and detrimental to the growth of personality when one becomes identified with it and imagines it to be the whole of oneself. This is not unusual; we are familiar enough with the business man who is still the business man when he comes home at night; the clerk who is clerkly with his intimate friends; the preacher who never leaves the pulpit; the actor who never leaves the stage. We have all been badly shaken when our own masks failed suddenly to convince, and we have been shocked to see a friend's mask stripped off, to see someone drastically different standing there. In either event we may shudder at the pretense—but wouldn't it be wiser to shudder at the confusion? The persona is necessary: we cannot walk around with naked souls in the world of action. We need simply to remember that neither we nor our fellow men are summed up by the mask we use to face the moment, we need to learn to expect and even to rely on the inconsistencies of human nature, the contradictions, the inevitable other side. We may then avoid being too shocked and shaken when the masks, including our own, suddenly crack.

The use of the persona is not restricted to one's dealings with the outer world. We turn it toward the inner world also, in the attempt to face down, to keep in the dark, whatever might be stirring there, in the realm of the shadow.

The concept of the shadow in analytical psychology is a good bit more elusive than the concepts of identification, anxiety and persona. This is true because it refers not only to realms of unconsciousness but, specifically, to what we do not wish to be conscious of. It strikes down to the level below our identifications and our masks, below our accepted ethics and moralities, where our most natural contradictions, oppositions and dualities are at work. The concept becomes much clearer if we remember that the psyche never ceases to strive for harmony and balance.

What lies in the realm of the shadow is all that is unrealized and undeveloped within each individual and all that is unacceptable and repressed according to his own intrinsic standards. To this extent, therefore, the shadow is *personal*—as though we ourselves, all unawares, had as we grew cast a lengthening, deepening shadow to conceal whatever we could not accept as part of us. Beyond this, it is the realm of partial and stunted growth, partial and neglected discovery, and the realm of the primal natural man, the old Adam; it shades into the black density of night, so to speak in the realm of the psyche's primordial inertia.

The shadow is a natural part of the inner world, as urgent with life as the rest of that world and as necessary to man in his wholeness, but it seems to us—as we function in the light of our partial awareness—to be unnatural, inimical, evil, full of death; and in our ignorance we add to it, making the dark darker so that we cannot see what might be hidden in it. It must seem to us a matter of self-preservation. Our immediate experience of the natural order, both inner and outer, proves it to be full of brutality, cruelty and destructiveness; from our own point of view, whether we encounter these facts in the world or in ourselves, they promise nothing but our annihilation. But we misunderstand the conditions of the psyche, misjudge what will preserve us and misapply our ethics and moralities. Clearly, the external world, apart from the actions of men within it, is beyond our judgment: it seems to turn and work, in the light of an all-encompassing Awareness, as much through death as through life, as much through destruction and decay, as through building and growth, its lively opposites seeming always complementary. The same is ultimately true of the inner world.

If we are to remain human and go further in our discovery of what being human may mean, then it is necessary to accept and endure the pain of knowing those things about ourselves which are neither godlike nor saintly nor good nor nice. They are as full of energy as their opposites, as the manure heap is as full of energy as the flowering tree. We have abundant proof of it in our history of the misuse of this energy: our inquisitions and witch hunts, our evangelical conquests, our racial, political and social purges and our righteous wars have demanded and squandered more energy than we ever imagined we could summon, or, at peace with one another, could ever conceivably need.

The concept of the shadow, and the "problem of evil" it represents, is fully explored from different perspectives in the discussions that follow about the Golden Calf, the Book of Job, the great stories of the Book of Genesis and, most intimately and directly, the case of Joan. I have dealt with it here in a preliminary way because—like identification, anxiety and persona—it is a natural part of the growth and development of the psyche and because it bears vitally upon my intellectual patient's questions about self-knowledge and *what* is to be known.

The Archetypes

ACCORDING to the myths of creation, out of the nebulous, everything came quickly: light and dark, heaven and earth, the firmament and the seas, animals and men. The inner world is brought into being as quickly as the outer and is active from the beginning. The infant seems to dream, as though even at that early stage, the waters scarcely divided, he were being informed as surely by the one world as the other. Past infancy, it is a matter of both worlds' being in action, reaction and interplay. We begin to act and react without ever having thought; we have thoughts and feelings out of nowhere; we are driven by forces we could never name, whose existence we never suspected. We go on dreaming and remember our dreams, and they are experiences often more vivid and real than any that happen in the light of day. We remember and forget, accept and reject, affirm and deny, as we move toward some sort of summation of *who* we are.

On a deeper level, we have without knowing it been doing the same thing—seeing, so to speak, feeling and acting in most meaningful ways. It is on this level below our immediate awareness that the persona is shaped and that our identifications come about; here, for example, we take the sour grapes into our mouths. And below this level lies the shadow, and below this there is more than we ever dreamed of—yet, through dreams, symbols and images we may come to know. In the inner world as in the outer there is first all that is personal and our own; beyond this, all that is impersonal, not our own but available to us; and beyond this, all that is transpersonal, belonging to all mankind from the beginning. This latter is the realm of the archetypes.

The word *archetype* is from the Greek *arche,* meaning first, foremost, chief (as seen in the familiar English prefix of archbishop, archangel, etc.), and *typos,* a blow or the mark left by a blow, an impress, or mold (as in type, typical, etc.). The word had great meaning for Ambrose and Tertullian and St. Augustine's "principales formae" is a rendering of the original *archetypoi:*

They themselves do not come into being or perish, but everything which does come into being or perishes is said to be formed according to them. . . . These primary things are not only ideas but are true, because they are eternal and because they remain the same and unchangeable. Through participation in them it happens that everything is what it is and how it is.[9]

The archetypes derive, then, from a realm far beyond the personal and particular. They are a manifestation of what Spinoza called *Substance,* in the sense that H. F. Hallett has defined it:

Substance as cause is absolutely free action or creation: it is not a "thing" but a self-realizing and self-manifesting *agency.* Modes as effects of that agency are created beings actualizing the potency of their cause.[10]

As used in analytical psychology, archetype is perhaps best defined as *master pattern.* Part of humanity's most remote heritage, modes of the psyche's action deeper than any other, the archetypes are patterns of *motivation* by which man's actions are unconsciously conditioned and they may be taken, therefore, as *a priori* categories, reaching back into levels of experience where man neither knows nor remembers.

The full meaning of the concept of archetypes may be grasped only through direct personal experience—existentially, as it were—but one may approach an understanding of it by considering its origins in analytical thought and by listening carefully to what very serious people have said about their own experience.

Describing the practical background out of which grew his fundamental assertions about archetypes, C. G. Jung wrote:

. . . I would like to give a brief description of how this discovery took place. I had often observed patients whose dreams pointed to a rich store of fantasy material. Equally, from the patients themselves I got the impression that they were stuffed full of fantasies without their being able to tell me just where the inner pressure lay. I therefore took up a dream image or an association of the patient's, and, with this as a point of departure, set him the task of elaborating or developing

33

his theme by giving free rein to his fantasy. . . . The result of this technique was a vast number of complicated patterns whose diversity puzzled me for years, until I was able to recognize that in this method I was witnessing the spontaneous manifestation of an unconscious process . . . to which I later gave the name "individuation process." . . . The more I suspected these patterns of harboring a certain purposefulness, the less inclined I was to risk any theories about them.

. . . The chaotic assortment of images that at first confronted me reduced itself in the course of the work to certain well-defined themes and formal elements which repeated themselves in identical or analagous form with the most varied individuals. . . .

. . . These experiences and reflections lead me to believe that there are certain collective unconscious conditions which act as *regulators and stimulators of creative fantasy activity* and call forth corresponding formations by availing themselves of the existing conscious material. They behave exactly like the motive forces of dreams, . . . [My italics.][11]

Neither the existence of the archetypes themselves nor our personal experience of them can be objectively proved, but there should be no real cause for alarm or skepticism in this. In the physical sciences we make constant use of such concepts as *electron* and *proton* that stand for entities that are not, of course, directly observable; the evidence of their existence derives from our observation of the phenomena they serve to explain. To ask what these concepts are is meaningless, for the only way to answer is not to *define* them but to *describe* them in terms of what has been observed. They are equated in fact with energy; and energy, as Bertrand Russell put it, ". . . is not defined except as regards its laws and the relation of changes in its distribution to our sensations . . ."[12] We know, in other words, of something we call energy, but we know of it only because we have inferred its existence from phenomena we have observed; and by further inference we accept the existence of complexes of energy we call protons, electrons, etc. By a similar process of thought (for it is, after all, the human mind studying manifestations of energy itself, whether in the outer world or the inner), we infer the existence of archetypes because they best explain certain psychic phenomena. They are themselves manifestations of energy in specific constellations, energy being understood here as an active substratum of all cosmic occurrences. As such, analytical psychology asserts that the archetypes are innate in the human psyche, that we inherit them as we inherit our "instinctual" modes of adaptation. Our gift for symbolization and imaging is, for example, a part of our archetypal heritage. Analytical psychology does not assert that the symbols themselves are inherited, but rather that the gift to symbolize and image, the urge to express that gift and the use the psyche makes of it, inhere in man *qua* man and are a part of *who* he is. The wide acceptance and use of particular symbols and their appearance as culturally conditioned variants in widely separated parts of the world simply indicates a general recognition of their adequateness to reveal something of the psychic experiences all men share.

The symbols by which the archetypes reveal their presence and their activity to our consciousness are infinitely varied: abstract or, to our feelings, concrete as can be; impersonal and very remote from any present situation, or very personal and very close; utterly foreign and strange, or as familiar as the figures and motifs of mythology and legend. As expressions of the archetypes, their quality is always transpersonal; but their motive is to *inform* the personal. The empirical interpretation of these symbols and images *in relation to the individual's immediate experience at the moment of their expression* may significantly serve to illuminate that experience in depth, to reveal the individual's basic psychological attitudes and motivations and also to reveal something of the disposition of the transpersonal itself. It is in this way, among others, that for the individual discovery of the truly moral, the truly ethical, the essentially valuable becomes possible.

The symbols are manifestations of the archetypes. The archetypes, as "principales formae," *are manifestations of Being. As such, they are beyond judgment, as far beyond any considerations of right and wrong, good and evil, as the forces of the physical world. It is entirely a question of how we stand as regards their*

35

forceful activity, whether as individuals we are related with it or driven by it, unawares.

A dream of a patient may help to illustrate all this:

"I am looking at a plate on which there are a lot of white squares, on which are pictures or designs or images of some kind. Some are banners waving in the wind, some beautifully colored designs, some like Chinese characters or Egyptian hieroglyphics. Then a voice tells me that these images can be translated into words and that I can do it. But there is a feeling that I must do it quickly. There is a feeling of imminent danger or catastrophe unless I translate these things quickly."

The archetype symbolizes itself in the various designs (the banners, hieroglyphics and calligraphy) and simultaneously produces a pressure—or, as the patient felt it, a sense of danger. The patient was in the midst of an encounter with an ethical issue that involved her whole future as a wife and as an artist. She was confronted, in other words, with the necessity to discover for herself, *out of her own individuality,* an essential value. At this critical juncture, the archetype asserted itself, emphasizing the seriousness of her immediate situation by stimulating the sense of danger, but at the same time *regulating* that situation toward rightness by lifting it up to be viewed in more than personal terms. The patient felt the dream as an inner directive of enormous power and conviction, and from it she was able to discover a criterion by which to choose and act.

We experience archetypal activity in ways other than dreams. In a recent lecture, Sir Kenneth Clark spoke of "moments of vision"[13] that may come to a painter or poet unpredictably, with amazing vividness, and dominate a whole work of art. He suggested that the clue to the compelling, all-embracing character of such an experience may be found in the feeling of *self-discovery* that accompanies it. The "moment of vision" is related, evidently, to something within us that, as Coleridge wrote, "already and forever exists."

> In looking at objects . . . as at yonder moon, dim glimmering through the dewy window-pane, I seem rather to be seeking, as it were *asking* for, a symbolical language for something within me that already and for ever exists, than observing anything new. Even when the

latter is the case, yet still I have always an obscure feeling, as if that new phenomenon were the dim awakening of a forgotten or hidden truth of my inner nature.[14]

Sir Herbert Read writes about the experience from a different perspective, and speaks of the "moment of originality."

> A sense of reality is a conquest, an advance from the chaos and confusion of an unintelligible world: a construction. The first order introduced into man's conception of the world was an aesthetic order—the order of ritual and myth. Later the intellect gradually made a selection of the totality—the part it can describe and measure—and gave it a more or less coherent unity, and called it science. The map is constantly enlarged: new details are filled in; but vast territories of space and time must still be marked "terra incognita." The sensibility plays like lightning over these dark abysses, and in the flashes gets a brief glimpse of the lineaments of the Unknown: the brief glimpse that is the artist's intuition, and which he then strives to communicate to us by the symbols he invents. That is the moment of originality— the moment in which we are made to realize the ethereal shimmering texture of music, the "shapes that haunt thought's wilderness" in poetry, the "beauty wrought out from within upon the flesh" of a painting. Poetry, painting, music—all these are arts or skills for raising the senses to that condition of insight in which the world is not transfigured but in which for the first time some aspect of it is revealed, or made real, and thereby, for human eyes, newly created, newly communicated. [15]

The situation of the scientist is much the same. His discovery (the discovery itself, not its detailed validation) is often experienced as a lightning flash, a revelation. If the instant of it and what came before could be analyzed, we should surely find that the whole apparatus of consciousness was in action: thought, memory, feeling, intuition and all the senses somehow lifted to that high intensity which makes insight possible. But it goes beyond this; in such moments the psyche acts *as a whole,* makes actual its

37

potential unity and by virtue of this achievement itself reveals to the individual another aspect of reality.

When our personal relations are truly open and reciprocal, it is possible for us to experience a moment of vision, of originality, like the artist's or scientist's—a kind of communication, almost a communion, that goes far beyond what could be mediated by the senses alone. The *validation* of such an experience must derive from our psychic situation at the moment of its happening; nevertheless, through it we may comprehend the essential of the other one—the *Thou**—in symbols and achieve a new field of awareness.

The whole psyche is more than the sum of its parts. When the psyche's potential wholeness and unity is made actual, it is in the *more,* the *plus,* that new fields of awareness are to be found; and the discovery of them has the compelling, numinous quality of "knowing" in the deepest sense. The act of discovery cannot be willed and it cannot be contrived; it can only be, on the individual's part, an act of true creativity.

These experiences and discoveries are brought about by the activity of an archetype that in analytical psychology is called the *Self.* Just as the physical organism in its development toward maturity and the harmonious working of all its parts has inherent in it, by some means eternally mysterious, a predetermined, ideal form, so too does the psyche in its own development—this is the Self. The Self is the ineffable center, but like the center of the onion it cannot be found, it is at once there and not there, and all is shaped around it.

The Self may be experienced in many different ways. It symbolizes itself in dreams as a circle, an inner eye, a mandala, a fountain or stream, or it may appear, by personification, in figures varying from the hermaphrodite to Christ. In all these varied symbols and images, two essential qualities may be discerned: wholeness, with all opposing forces reconciled; and at the same time an intrinsic openness—rounded, unified, yet open, precisely as the universe seems to be. What is flat, dimensional, delimited by time and space gives way to the rounded and harmoniously revolving whole; this is the ultimate sense of the archetype Self.

* See Martin Buber, *I and Thou* (New York, Charles Scribner's Sons).

Its activity asserts the relations of all things and all experience and is, therefore, the master pattern according to which personality develops.

One of my patients dreamed:

"I find a suitcase in a room and in it is an entire set of clothes. Everything I need is there—not too much and not too little. Someone tried to persuade me to get other new things, but when I look into the suitcase I know that anything more would be superfluous. A new kind of rhythm seems to have come to me. It doesn't come from outside, nor has it anything to do with opinions of what is right and wrong. I see it as a gold-colored stream, flowing, its pressure is constant, but according to what it has to meet its course changes. I know that if I can only keep in contact with the stream, things will go well with me; but if I let my attention be drawn and influenced by outside people and events and react without the new rhythm—the awareness of the stream—I shall get hopelessly lost."

This dream reveals the archetype Self in action, simultaneously complementing and strengthening the personality. It asserts a condition of unity yet defines that condition as open, rhythmic, flowing, and insists on the basis of it that things may go well or badly as the dreamer chooses. But now she *may* choose, and choose rightly, for the dream has shown her in the most explicit symbolic terms a way of right relation with her experience.

If we are to have criteria for action such as this dream gave the dreamer, standards by which to judge and a sense not only of values but of the value of values, we must discover them through our experience of and our relation with those forces of our being that are other than personal. Otherwise our ethics and morality will spring from personal considerations, and they in turn will spring from our identifications and our limitations, so that in the long run our choices and our actions will reflect our unconsciousness. A free and responsible decision, ultimately a *human* decision, must necessarily spring from our awareness of and our relations with those deep forces at work within the psyche that serve to determine our direction. It is impossible, therefore, to insist too much upon the importance of the archetypes, of which the Self is an example.*

* Here, as elsewhere, I differ from the "orthodox" Jungian position. I do not consider the shadow and the persona as archetypes; they are acquired faculties of the psyche.

39

I have been speaking here of the archetypes primarily in their positive effects. Like all other forces, they may have negative effects as well. The obvious present trend toward totalitarianism, even among the "free" societies, is, I suggest, the result of the activity of the archetype Self. Such manifestation is a monstruous distortion of the archetype of wholeness, but that is how we experience it now—and that, in turn, is the result of our present conception of what man as Man truly is.

If we believe that a man is merely the product of the past, the environment and the society, we automatically reduce him to the level of the primitive. On that level he cannot cooperate humanly with his environment or his society because he is contained within them, exactly as his primitive ancestors were contained within the natural order, driven and haunted, utterly lacking in personality. In such a condition man's thinking becomes alogical; he falls into moral insensitivity, then into moral stupor. His lack of relation with inner experience is quickly and perfectly reflected in his lack of relation to the organs of government. He allows himself simply to be ruled. Yet the archetypes continue to be active within him. The psyche's urge, governed by the Self, to achieve its potential wholeness emerges in warped, distorted and inhuman ways —in projections, for example, of the identity itself onto the mechanisms, conventions and ambitions of the state.

The present human condition indicates a containment on the part of vast numbers of people within the archetype Self. We lack any awareness of it and of what it represents as a direct manifestation of Being—as the true source, in fact, of moral, ethical, human values.

Any state of containment is a violation of Being itself. Every truly moral decision, every truly moral action—or omit the word *moral* and say simply that every decision and every action that affirms *life,* not death, *creativity,* not inertia, depends on individual freedom, not only political freedom but in particular *psychological* freedom, and this consists precisely and exclusively in the experience of the relations of things and of our human distinction in the midst of them.

Who is the knower? *Who* is it who is to be free?

The question is beyond a rational answer for the very reason that it asks *who,* not what. The human being is biologically a thing, a *what,* and he may psychically be a thing in his fixed attitudes, his identifications, his unshakable prejudices, his inertia; but his human essence is to be found elsewhere, in his unique situation in regard to the orders of experience. It is perhaps in this that we are made "in the image and likeness of God."

What is to be known?

Clearly, there is no limit to that question's answer. From the narrow confines of our identifications and our masks to the expanses of the realms of the shadow and of the archetypes, to the world of our own individuality: the frontiers are unimaginable.

What is Psychotherapy?

LIKE MANY other people (though they would not put it this way nor, in the long run, even be conscious of it), my intellectual patient had entered the psychotherapeutic situation in search of an authority outside himself. He shared the popular delusion that psychotherapy means to be the new authority, replacing all those others that have lost their spell, and that it has so established itself. Nothing in our first meetings disturbed him so much as my assertion that this is not true. He knew that it was necessary to make a distinction between psychology and psychotherapy. The former, as a science, seeks to arrive at universally valid laws, with as objective an attitude as possible. And the latter? Wasn't it a reliable medical process, having proven techniques for the diagnosis of his ailment and for its cure? If not, then, as he said, what was he doing in my office?

Psychotherapy is a participation of two (or more) psychic systems in a process of events. It is a *reciprocal relationship,* an interaction, as it were, of psychic systems upon each other, and it has as its aim to assist in the growth of personality and thus ultimately to assist the individual toward the realization of his potential wholeness.

If this is true, to what extent is the scientific goal of objectivity achievable in the psychotherapeutic situation? Jung says:

> A person is a psychic system which, when it affects another person, enters into a reciprocal reaction with another psychic system. This, perhaps the most modern, formulation of the psychotherapeutic relation between physician and patient, is clearly very far removed from the original view that psychotherapy was a method which anybody could apply in stereotyped fashion in order to reach the desired result.[16]

This statement casts a direct light upon the question of why there are different schools of this relatively new "science" of the psyche. Each of these schools is, in effect, founded upon a *projection onto objectivity* of a particular set of interests and values held by a particular scientist or group of scientists. Since the physician's own psychic system is so directly and intimately involved with the patient's, absolute statements of "pure objectivity" about the individual psyche *as a whole* are out of the question. So-called objective, scientific statements, therefore, relate at best only to those parts of the psychic system that may in fact be amenable to comparison and statistical measurement; they do not and cannot relate to that part of the psychic system that is individual and unique. In psychotherapy we are confronted by a paradox: the individual signifies nothing in comparison with the universal; the universal signifies nothing in comparison with the individual. For the physical scientist, applying his methods, there is an obvious Archimedean point outside his situation, relative to which his statements become meaningful. For the psychotherapist, that Archimedean point is missing and must each time, in each daily encounter with each patient, be discovered. As Harry Stack Sullivan once wrote:

> The processes and the changes in processes that make up the data which can be subjected to scientific study occur, not in the subject person nor in the observer, but in the *situation* which is created between the observer and his subject.[17]

In psychotherapy, in other words, knowledge (whether it

may be subjected to "scientific" study or not) is arrived at and the meaningful discovered out of the relationship itself. But the fundamental principle is the same for psychotherapy as for the physical sciences. It could not, at bottom, be otherwise, for man is involved, committed to the search for truth. The essence of the method used in science is to refer the restricted certainty outward into the unrestricted void, and thus farther and farther to comprehend. In psychotherapy, what is being referred is human experience; the field of that referral is the situation of the patient and the therapist; the objective standard and guide by which the referral is made is discovered and developed out of the human relationship itself.

The psychotherapist who conceives the situation in this way cannot approach it as the adherent of any absolute doctrine and cannot treat each patient by the same fixed method. He must instead participate in a process of growth. Since there is infinite variety in individuality and in individual experience and relations, he has no grounds for pretending to superior knowledge. Certainly the depth of his knowledge of himself, the quality and scope of his training and of his experience as a therapist and as a human being are of enormous importance, not because they equip him to instruct his patient, but because they inform his moral sensitivity, and it is this that determines the quality of the atmosphere in which growth is to take place. There is no occasion for instruction of the patient; there is no teaching and, in the situation as described, no question of doctrinal compliance. Neither is there, on the therapist's part, any occasion for judgment on moral or ethical grounds. This would imply anarchy, an atmosphere of laissez faire close to absurdity, if it were not that the key to the situation is the human relationship itself. This is the governing principle, and without the experience of it there can be no growth.

These days, we cannot get at the true meaning of the phrase *human relationship* without a careful re-examination of what it seems to refer to in our own experience and of what it implies beyond our personal experience. Obviously on the biological level it is the *sine qua non:* immediate survival depends upon a system of relations that sustain us. We are dependent in our physical existence, from the beginning: dependent upon others, upon the natural order and increasingly upon ourselves. Out of this last dependence we come slowly to a sense, uniquely human, of independence in *being*. It is then that the world's oppositions and the dualities and paradoxes of life really begin to be felt. Mythology expresses this primal fact, need and experience in such symbols as the "Great Mother" and "Great Father," figures at once benevolent and malign, positive and negative, constructive and destructive: naturally so, since the dichotomy of *independence in being* and *dependence in physical existence* is at the heart of all human relationships. This explains why the psychotherapist is so particularly interested in the patient's past relations, especially those of his childhood: they indicate simultaneously the modes of his dependence and of his independence, the status of his developing personality as it reveals itself at every turn under the impact of what, out of his intrinsic individuality, he chose and did not choose to be related with. But to get at the deepest meaning of human relationship, we must go to a level beyond personal need and intimate past experience, a level beyond choice, so to speak—which yet, paradoxically, is the ground of choice.

According to our perceptions, directed by our sense of independence in being, we are isolated from the natural world, from our fellowmen and somehow from ourselves as well. The inner and outer worlds seem to be opposites: the one existing in time and space and subject to all the laws and distresses of matter; the other timeless and spaceless, swept by the windy distresses of the immaterial, the spiritual. This seems to be the true state of things, but is it really so? Modern science has revised its concept of the physical world as a structure existing in time and space independent of the observer.* We have found ourselves capable of experi-

---

* "The modern astrophysical world view, which began with Galileo, and its challenge to the adequacy of the senses to reveal reality, have left us a universe of whose qualities we know no more than the way they affect our measuring instruments, and—in the words of Eddington—'the former have as much resemblance to the latter as a telephone number has to a subscriber.' Instead of objective qualities, in other words, we find instruments, and instead of nature or the universe—in the words of Heisenberg—'man encounters only himself.' . . .

"With the rise of modernity, mathematics does not simply enlarge its content or reach out into the infinite to become applicable to the immensity of an infinite and infinitely growing, expanding universe, but

ences which seem to indicate that space, as well as time, is a category of the intellect, and we have found it necessary virtually to abandon the concept *matter* since we accepted the wave equation in dealing with electrons. We find it, therefore, impossible to say now whether the physical world is after all intrinsically different from the world of the psyche. In the final analysis, it seems that we talk about two orders of experience. The nearer we come to fullness of personality, to an expansive means of relation with both these orders of experience, the more surely do we sense that our true identity resides at the ineffable point at which these orders converge, intermingle and lose their seeming opposition. Then the way lies open for the experience of the Self in its essence as the archetype of relationship. The Self accepts life *as a whole* and allows all experience, and when we are properly related with it, it acts within the psyche always in favor of wholeness, the unified, rounded, harmonious, yet open and free. According to our willingness to accept and allow in the same way, we may come to that signal experience of the inescapable relations of all things which turns independence in being into dependence upon Being, dependence in physical existence into a relative freedom; for it is this experience which makes actual to us our unity within ourselves, with our fellow men and with the universe.

A *human* relationship becomes, therefore, potentially more than a personal, private matter. It is a way of experiencing and exemplifying in action an essential aspect of Being. It may, in other words, achieve *form,* in the artist's sense of that word. The power in the work of art that renders chaos into order, establishes dependencies in the name of independence, reconciles opposing forces in the name of a higher unity and itself continues to endure within that unity is, ultimately, the power of Being itself. It may equally infuse the relations of man with his fellow men.

It is this form that both patient and therapist may experience in their relationship. Though the therapist's participation has the quality of compassionate detachment, he must in fact take part

---

ceases to be concerned with appearances at all. It is no longer the beginning of philosophy, of the 'science' of Being in its true appearance, but becomes instead the science of the structure of the human mind." Hannah Arendt, *The Human Condition* (Chicago, The University of Chicago Press, 1958), pp. 261, 266.

45

not only as an observer but as a human being. Both he and the patient must make a mutual effort at adventurous human understanding; both set out together on a kind of voyage of exploration of the psyche. As the situation between them becomes more open and reciprocal, they are both brought to deal with essentially unconscious material; and when that material is of a transpersonal nature, both may experience the human relationship at its profoundest level, experience the Self as a direct manifestation of Being and discover much that is meaningful for all men.

The vital daily work of the psychotherapist comes to a focus in and must take its directive from the relations *of* experience and the patient's relations *to* experience. The crux of any human situation lies here. It is only the rarest among us who can find identity and true creativity in the deserts of isolation.

One of my patients dreamed:

"There is a man, and he seems to have the word or thought or something. He hands it to a man behind him, and this man hands it to one behind him, and so on and on. It seems as though this word is handed from one to another and back and back through time until it comes to what seems to be an animal. This animal then takes the word and hands it to the person in front of him, and he to the next in front of him, and on and on until it reaches the original person. Then this word has become something else—a knowledge this man did not have before. I watch all this and am very fascinated and excited over the process. I want to do this too, but now a voice warns me. It says: 'If one should try by onself, one could send the word as far as the animal, but there it would blow up and cause a great deal of trouble.' "

This dream expresses with great clarity the nature of the psychotherapeutic situation and what happens in it, but it speaks also about the human situation in general: one man needs the other if the potentialities of man himself are to be realized. It is best, therefore, that the patient continue to take part so far as he is able in the affairs of the world; he must continue to *live* his life outside of as well as inside the psychotherapeutic relationship. As he begins to emerge from his containment within the forces of the natural order, he finds himself able to step forward out of the frames of his various identifications, out of those strictures and limitations of individuality that in his inertia he has chosen or unwittingly accepted. His sense of himself, of *who* he is, is broadened and deepened. He becomes more willing to accept the *security of change* in place of the *insecurity of stasis*. He becomes more resilient in his summation of himself, more willing to allow what he might previously have rejected and denied, more willing to accept as part of his own nature whatever he might encounter in the voyage he has undertaken.

Faith is not required for this voyage, nor is belief: the very nature of the situation rules out any question of psychotherapy as a new authority. All that is necessary in the beginning is a simple admission by the patient that what he knows of himself is perhaps not all there is to be known; that his summation of himself is partial and that he might find something of value in what is missing. He should throughout be as open as he possibly can, yet he should be *guarded* in his openness, for it is only he, as an individual, who can find the way to his wholeness. A *guarded openness* will sustain him in the beginning, but beyond this it is an inner resolution that will make him persist.

The farther he is able to go in this voyage of discovery, the more he is willing to allow as truly himself, the more the primal waters divide, uncovering new ground, making space where there was none before. This new space is vital: neither growth nor change can come about when there is no room. More and more of what has been repressed and unconscious may be brought up into this new space, may be looked at and integrated with the developing personality. In psychotherapy this is the healing process. It does not happen unless the situation itself is so open as to allow the patient freely to express *all* his feelings, whether positive or negative, constructive or destructive; nor does it happen unless the relationship between him and the therapist is *in its quality* symbolic of what all his relations with all his experience might come to be.

But according to what principles does this healing process take place? According to what wisdom? The dream quoted directly above suggests the answers to these questions: the key is in the "animal." There is, in the Old Testament, a dramatic incident that also concerns an "animal" and that reveals with perfect precision and simplicity, but in terms of the poetic symbol, the primary task between patient and therapist and the way by which they may fulfill it. The characters, setting and action are integral parts of a whole and remarkable symbol. In the realization of it *as a whole,* the poets confront a deep and abiding psychological problem and show its consequences; state the human measures to be taken in dealing with it, and show those measures in action. The wisdom is implicit in the resolution. Much of modern psychotherapeutic practice has been based upon it.

The Golden Calf

THE ISRAELITES had been freed from bondage in Egypt; the period of their preparation for the reception of the Law had ended, and they were gathered at Sinai. Moses left them and went up the Mount to receive the Law.

> And when the people saw that Moses delayed to come down out of the mount, the people gathered themselves together unto Aaron, and said unto him, Up, make us gods, which shall go before us; for as for this Moses, the man that brought us up out of the land of Egypt, we wot not what is become of him.
>
> Exodus, 32:1

> And Moses turned and went down from the mount, and the two tables of the testimony were in his hand: the tables were written on both their sides; on the one side and on the other were they written.
> And the tables were the work of God, and the writing was the writing of God, graven upon the tables.
> And when Joshua heard the noise of the people as they shouted, he said unto Moses, There is a noise of war in the camp.
> And he said, It is not the voice of them that shout for mastery, neither is it the voice of them that cry for being overcome: but the noise of them that sing do I hear.

And it came to pass, as soon as he came nigh unto the camp, that he saw the calf, and the dancing: and Moses' anger waxed hot, and he cast the tables out of his hands, and brake them beneath the mount.

And he took the calf which they had made, and burnt it in the fire, and ground it to powder, and strawed it upon the water, and made the children of Israel drink of it.

And Moses said unto Aaron, What did this people unto thee, that thou hast brought so great a sin upon them?

And Aaron said, Let not the anger of my lord wax hot; thou knowest the people, that they are set on mischief.

For they said unto me, Make us gods, which shall go before us: for as for this Moses, the man that brought us up out of the land of Egypt, we wot not what is become of him.

And I said unto them, Whosoever hath any gold, let them break it off. So they gave it me: then I cast it into the fire, and there came out this calf.*

Exodus, 32:15–24

The drama begins when authority has lost its spell. The moment is highly complex. After the bondage in Egypt, there had been a long hiatus in the desert, a time of wandering led by Moses who, as leader, held whatever authority there was; now the hiatus was ending, a new freedom coming, shaped by a new and higher authority that would reveal itself on Mount Sinai. It is a very human and critical moment, and in the critical moment nothing is ever certain: everything gained may on the instant be lost, and the whole of the future may go one way or the other, depending. Moses did not come back in good time from the mountain top; no one knew what had become of him; his spell as a leader dwindled. He might be lost, might never return: for his people, what might be, suddenly became fact. They fell back at once upon their primitive ways, lapsing into that state of mind that can only grasp and

* Rashi, in his commentary, renders this: "I cast it into the fire, I did not know that the Calf would come out, *it fashioned itself.*"

49

follow the visible concrete sign: "Make us gods which shall go before us." What had they followed through the desert and the time of trial: the Word or the man who spoke it? Once he is lost, the Word itself is lost. Now, if the gods exist, a man must make them and set them up on earth to be touched, looked at, danced around. Aaron gave in to them, and they brought their gold, their treasure, what they valued most, and threw it into the fire. Then the miracle happened: out of the flames leaped the Golden Calf.[18]

Why a calf? The calf was a symbol of the earth and of fertility. Osiris, the corn god, and Mithras, the god of nature, were worshiped in the form of a calf or bull. The early Christian writers often mention the identification of the Golden Calf with the Egyptian god, Apis. Jewish legends add the following:

> Amongst the ornaments and rings which the people brought to Aaron, he found a ring, on the one side of which was inscribed the Holy Name, but on its other, the image of a calf. This earring he threw into the fire and thereupon out came the calf bleating and was seen by Israel.[19]

And:

> Micha of Mount Ephraim, a wonder worker, came there and cast into the fire a little tablet on which were written the words: "Arise thou bull." This however Moses had thrown into the Nile when he fetched Joseph's coffin out of the Nile. Immediately the calf came out of the fire bleating and leaping.[20]

Legendary material like this, both Jewish and Christian, is full of meaning, and it will be used and referred to throughout this book. It shows the response of later generations to the original event, proves the power and liveliness of the original symbol as it continues to stir the deep energies of the psyche. If we were as open, our own energies might be stirred in the same way, to a similar depth of insight into the laws of the inner world.

Two highly important motifs are added to the original incident by the legends just quoted: the "Holy Name" inscribed on the ring and the words "Arise thou bull" on the tablet; and the motif of Joseph who was "the firstling of the bullock." The first is the principle of the Word, as in Genesis; the Word of Spirit which, when uttered, stirs an element of chaos and shapes it into a perceptible and meaningful form. It is the *word* in its ultimate sense: the seed holding hidden within itself the future whole, the fully developed and rounded thing. As a principle, it is here intimately connected with the motif of Joseph who, before he died, made the Israelites swear to carry his bones with them out of Egypt.

> Many relate that a metal coffin was prepared for Joseph and sunk in the Nile. What actually took place? At first Joseph's body was buried in a field and the field was extremely fertile. When this was noticed, the body was stolen and buried in another field and again the field yielded richer fruit than before. The news of this finally reached Pharaoh, whose wise man said: "The Egyptians are all nourished by the waters of the Nile, and hence we will sink him in the river that it may be blessed for his sake." And the Egyptians made a metal coffin for Joseph's remains and sank them in the river in order that the land should never again be visited by famine.[21]

"How did Moses know where Joseph was buried?" it is asked in the Talmud.

> It is related that Sera, the daughter of Aser, one of that generation, had remained behind and Moses went to her and asked if she knew where Joseph was buried. She answered him: "The Egyptians made for him a metal coffin and sank it into the Nile in order that its waters be blessed." Whereupon Moses went unto the banks of the Nile and said: "Joseph, the time has come with regard to which you made us swear. If you now appear, it is good; if not, then we are released from our oath." In that hour Joseph's coffin appeared and Moses took it and had it carried with him. Throughout all the years the Israelites wandered in the desert, these two boxes, the one the coffin of the dead, and the other, the ark of the divine, were carried side by side, and strangers often asked the meaning of these boxes. To

whom the Israelites replied: "The one is that of a dead man, the other that of the divine." And when they asked: "Is it seemly that a dead man should travel beside the divine?" they received the answer: "The one fulfilled all that is written in the other."[22]

Joseph was the master of dreams: his ears had been opened in his deep sleep and his instruction sealed. He knew the earth at first hand, having been cast down into it by his brothers when he was a child. As interpreter of Pharoah's dreams, he knew the numinous power of the calf as symbol and he had taken that power into himself and could give it back again, symbolically, to save his own people and to make fertile the land of Egypt. There is a subtle interplay of opposites here: on the one hand the calf as idol, on the other the calf as symbol; on the one hand the Israelites lapsed into primitivity, capable suddenly of grasping nothing but the visible sign; on the other, Joseph in all his awareness, an awareness that continues symbolically in its full power and vitality long after his death and burial under the waters of the Nile—the Word did not escape him. For the psyche, Joseph emerges as symbolic of what the Israelites, on the very brink of freedom and at the very moment of receiving the Law, are in mortal danger of losing. When Moses steps into the idolatrous scene, it is not only a matter of opposites in subtle interplay, but of irony of majestic proportions.

He, God's anointed, came down from the Mount with the Tables of the Law in his hands. It was the moment of his glory; he had fulfilled himself. If his people were on the brink, he had already stepped over; what they were prepared for, he had already received. He heard the noise, saw the dance, and he smashed the Tables of the Law on the rock, burned up the Calf, ground the ashes to powder, scattered them on the waters and made the Israelites drink the mixture.

> In the hour [the legend says] when Moses broke the tables of the covenant, the waters of the ocean overflowed its banks and wished to flood the world. Thereupon Moses took the calf and burned it. Then he called unto the waters: "O Waters, what are you about?" The ocean answered: "The world could only exist in virtue

of the Law which was written on the tables. But the Law was betrayed by the children of Israel when they made the golden calf, so we shall destroy the world." Thereupon Moses said: "So be it; may all those who have committed this sin be handed over to you." And he strewed the ashes on the sea. But the sea still did not grow calm. Then Moses mixed the water with the ashes of the golden calf and gave it to the children of Israel to drink. Immediately the wrath of the ocean was appeased.[23]

The waters are an ancient symbol of the primal realm of the psyche; drinking and eating are ancient symbols of spiritual assimilation, that is, *integration*. What really happened was that the Israelites received the *whole* of God's Law.

In the legend, the waters raged not because the Tables of the Law had been shattered, but because the Israelites had already broken the Law before its literal breaking ever took place. The irony is compounded, and in opposite directions. By their literal dance, the Israelites violated a symbol and proved that the true language of the Law (the Word) was beyond their understanding. But the waters did not rage until Moses, by a literal act, broke the Law to bits. There is a hint here that the children of Israel might, in their wrong-headedness, have been right; that authority needed, at least at this critical moment, to lose its spell, for there would be meaning in the loss. By his literal act, Moses himself steps down into confusion.

He had done it before. There is a key to his character in the way he called out to the dead Joseph from the banks of the Nile: if the great fertile symbol did not reappear there and then, he would be free of his oath. Later, in the desert, when there was no water and God commanded him to *speak* to the rock, he doubted and instead of the Word he used his magic rod, and because of that God exiled him forever from the Promised Land.[24]

A legend pictures Moses at the rock, with the people gathered around him, saying to himself:

"If I now speak to the rock, bidding it bring forth water, and it bring forth none, I shall subject myself to humiliation in the presence of the community, for they will say, 'Where is thy wisdom?' " Hence he said to the people: "Ye know that God can perform miracles for ye, but He hath hidden from me out of which rock He will let the water flow forth. For whenever the time comes that God wishes a man not to know, then his wisdom and understanding are of no avail to him." Moses then lifted his rod and let it quietly slide down upon the rock upon which he laid it, uttering, *as if addressing Israel,* the words, "Shall we bring you forth water out of this rock?" The rock of its own accord now began to give forth water, whereupon Moses struck upon it with his rod, but then the water no longer flowed forth, but blood. Moses thereupon said to God: "This rock brings forth no water," and God instantly turned to the rock with the question: "Why dost thou bring forth not water, but blood?" The rock answered: "O Lord of the world! Why did Moses smite me?" When God asked Moses why he had smitten the rock, he replied: "That it might bring forth water." God, however, said to Moses: "Had I bidden thee to smite the rock? I had only said, Speak to it." Moses tried to defend himself by saying, "I did speak to it, but it brought forth nothing."

God chastised him and told him his punishment ("Neither thou, nor thy brother, nor thy sister shall set foot upon the land of Israel."), then God turned to the rock, saying, " 'Turn thy blood into water,' and so it came to pass."[25]

Moses was a rational man: time and circumstance may limit an oath and even relieve one of the burden of it; water does not come from rocks, that kind of transubstantiation does not happen by the power of the Word alone. His rage at the sight of the Golden Calf was also rational, or at least reasonable: the Law was in his hands, written by God on solid stone, for his people to read. It is reasonable that, in his rage at finding them unworthy, the *symbol* of the Law in his mind should become the *idol* of the Law in his hand and that he should vengefully shatter it. Then he destroyed the Calf. But after this he began to act in ways that were unlike him. It was not rational to scatter the ashes on the water, and certainly it was not rational to force the Israelites to drink the ferment. These are things Joseph, not Moses, would naturally have done, for they involve action with the *true substance* directly, with the Word and not with the rod. This is the crux of the irony.

At the critical moment for the Israelites, God intervenes not only on the mountain top, as He hands down the Law, but also on the plain below. There, out of the primal realms of the psyche, called by the Word as the water was called from the rock, the Calf leaps forth, a symbol of the fruitful earth, seemingly an idol, truly an idol to both the Israelites and to Moses. But, in reality, in its connection with Joseph it is a symbol of man's unity with the natural order. It was this side of man's existence and this unity that Moses, in his metaphysical ecstasy, was about to forget and that his people in their primitive frenzy had betrayed, for it is a unity that depends upon distinction within the natural order—upon relationship—and not submersion in it. The waters of the mind raged, the legend says: they always do when the inner weather is made turbulent by the unassimilated, the rejected, the overemphasized and idolized. Scattering the ashes did not calm them, and Moses tried again, acting in a way that must have been utterly mysterious to his rational mind, inspired out of a region of himself he knew little of. Joseph would have understood immediately. The people drank the ferment of water and ash, and the waters themselves grew calm. In this way the people exemplified in symbolic action the reception of the Law and they did, in reality, receive the *whole* of it at this moment: the "Word" *and* the "Calf" in their true unity.

> God said to Moses on the Mount: "Moses, you can only see one vision, but I see two visions. You see them coming to Sinai and receiving My Law and so do I. This, however, is only one vision. But I can also see the vision of the Golden Calf, as it is said: *I have seen this peo-ple.*"[26]

It is in the symbolic drinking of the water and ash that psychotherapy finds a mode of treatment, a way of dealing with the problems of modern man as they present themselves in all their kaleidoscopic subtlety. Modern psychology has taught us beyond any question that suppression of the facts and denial of the readiness and willingness to do a certain deed achieves nothing; noth-

Figure 3.
The Candlestick of the Tabernacle supported by the Beast

ing, that is, but conflict between the natural forces of the inner world, bringing sickness and perhaps death to the personality. The Israelites were still capable of idolatry—they carried the idol itself, the bull of Egypt, unawares in the depths of the psyche—and a moment of readiness was all that was necessary to let it leap forth, an impossible god but a vital, fruitful symbol when joined with the Word. In our dreams and fantasies and at moments in our waking life, the Word sounds and what springs forth, as the Calf sprang from the fire, must be dealt with. As Moses learned, it is not enough to destroy it; to scatter it, *to analyze it away,* is not enough either. The healing comes with the "drinking down" of what certainly does most often seem a poisonous brew.

In my patient's dream, the psyche itself views the process of healing from a different angle: the "word" is passed back "through time," from the light of consciousness through varying shades of darkness to the night of the "animal," the *not yet human,* deep within, and the "animal" returns it, passing it back to the light where it emerges as the "Word," the new knowledge no man had before. But it all depends on the "other," on the experience of relationship. If this is lacking, the "word" explodes.

The idea of transformation is central to the paradoxical incident at Sinai. The people brought their hoarded gold and cast it into the fire; and what leaped out was something they thought they would treasure more than gold, since they had sacrificed gold for the higher good that would come with the presence of the god. The gold was transformed into the "god," but his glittering shape stood for a mortal danger and Moses knew it, seeing as he did with his people's eyes. He was an idolator himself, but of a far more subtle variety. The legend does not say, nor does the Old Testament, that he drank the ferment: evidently he did not need to, since by the mixing of it he had exemplified the Law in action. His casting of the ashes on the water was, in a sense, as primitive an act as the dance around the calf. The Bull of Adonis was regularly cast into the sea by his worshipers, so that the sea could give birth to him again; it was a rite of resurrection. Then Joseph was cast into the Nile in a metal coffin, for reasons equally primitive, but now it is a question of *what* is being cast: on the one hand a literal idol; on the other, a man who had fulfilled the promise of the divine. Moses's act is, therefore, immediately one step removed from idolatry as far as history is concerned, and even further removed as far as Moses is concerned, in that he did it at all.

The final step is taken with the drinking of the ferment: the rite of resurrection becomes a rite of transformation. The pagan's Eternal Round is broken. Adonis as the bull symbolized the divine principle of fertility and creativity; Joseph was the man who had known the workings of that principle in all its mysterious ways. At Sinai the two are brought together and reconciled with each other and with their opposites in a whole symbol that—by the very fact that the poets were able to create it—reveals that the human psyche itself had achieved a new and vastly significant stage in its ontogenesis.

There had been within the psyche a more critical bondage than any the Israelites had suffered in Egypt, and it was immediately manifested in their quick readiness to lapse into primitivity. It is clear that the bonds were those of inertia: idolatry is inertia's flower, since the power, the force, the truth and the responsibility are imagined to have their source in the idol itself, the inert mass. Neither the Israelites nor Moses could be prepared for the reception of the Law until they had confronted this fact of their inner world. At the critical moment, the psyche itself, in its urge to wholeness and by virtue of its relationship with Being, produced, as it does in dreams, the visible sign of that condition within it that would forever stand against the reception of the Law. The forces of creativity collided with the forces of inertia, struck directly through the pagan round to its center, and the Calf leaped forth as the image of that which, as *center* and *hub,* had kept vital energies bound and forever circling. It is an amazing evocation: the Calf as idol reveals a fatal inertia, but as symbol it reveals and asserts the very opposite, the energy and fertility and creativity of the inner world. Juxtaposed against it, as the incident reaches its climax, is another symbol that, in the circumstances, is being brought down to, tending toward, a state of idolatry: in the dramatic instant as the Old Testament poets render it, the Tables of the Law and the Golden Calf are of equal stature. Both the stone tables and the golden idol are destroyed so that both may be truly assimilated, so that out of the assimilation *transformation* may take place. In their vision of the necessary ritual act that will make

Figure 4. The Madonna and the Beast

transformation possible, these poets prove again the remarkable depth of their insight into the nature of man. Whether we are conscious of it or not, it is this very depth and quality of insight throughout the Bible that impels us toward it and makes it hold the Western imagination as no other book is able to do.

The ritual drinking of the ferment of water and ash did not end for all time the idolatry of the Israelites. Long after, in the time of Sennacherib, they offered sacrifices to the Nehustan, the bronze serpent Moses had made in the desert, and Hezekiah the King, doing "that which was right in the sight of the Lord," had to break it to pieces.[27]

Ritual gives *form* to the possible, the potential, but no more than that. Action, the true assimilation, must follow if transformation is to take place.

My patient's dream was *ritualistic* in this sense: through it, in response to the psychotherapeutic situation, the inner world suggested the *form* of healing, the way by which it might be accomplished and, in doing so, answered the question, "What is psychotherapy?"

Like the symbolic incident of the Golden Calf, the dream insists on the principle of relationship and on the existence and significance of the natural order within the psyche. It insists that both are necessary if transformation is to take place. Or we may say that the dream itself is an expression of the archetype Self, which never ceases to work for harmony and wholeness within the inner world. In the figure of the "animal" the natural order is asserted, juxtaposed against the "word" in a position of equal value. The "word," the literal and rational and explainable, must be referred to the natural order if knowledge is to be transformed. The "animal" is, in fact, symbolic of what the natural order within the psyche ideally does. But it cannot do it without the "word"; the intellect and the gift of reason are as necessary, as indispensable, as all the other attributes that make us human. Neglect or deny a single one of them, and the specific energies by which it might have been manifested simply circle back upon themselves in an eternal round. The "word" and the "animal" are brought together, the vital process is accomplished, on the basis of the relations of things, and out of the experience of relationship itself.

My patient's dream, in saying all this, emerges as a direct manifestation of archetypal activity aimed at regulating and directing the forces of the inner world toward an immediate goal of transformation and the final goal of wholeness. Yet it remains ritualistic. The question is always whether action will follow revelation.

Psychotherapy has come into being as a means of assisting in this activity and in the achievement of this goal. It can do no more and should aspire to do no less. As a human situation, it must affirm the relations of things and ultimately refer all things and all experience to the fact of Being. Out of this affirmation and this referral, meaningful action may proceed.

At Sinai Moses climbed back to the mountain top and begged forgiveness for his people, and soon after the Lord came down and spoke to him out of a cloudy pillar at the tabernacle door. Moses answered, "I beseech thee, show me thy glory." He had not changed; he still required the visible sign and proof of the invisible and unprovable. The Lord answered him: "Thou canst not see my face; for there shall no man see my face and live." Then the Lord commanded him to return to the mount.

> And he was there with the Lord forty days and forty nights; he did neither eat bread, nor drink water. And he wrote upon the tables the words of the covenant, the ten commandments.
>
> And it came to pass, when Moses came down from mount Sinai with the two tables of testimony in Moses' hand, when he came down from the mount, that Moses wist not that the skin of his face shone while he talked with him.
>
> Exodus, 34:28–29

On Dreams

THERE ARE as many kinds of dreams as there are individuals to dream them. Each is an experience in and of itself and of the instant. The meaning of a dream, like the meaning of an experience in the outer world, may be confined to the instant or may refer beyond it to the day's periphery, or to the year's, or far beyond to the timeless. One of the major achievements of psychology is that it has found ways to help the individual to understand his dreams; to see why he acts as he does in them, experiences what he experiences, why they are what they are and how they came to be that way. It is vital that he *should* understand his dreams, because they provide a direct and immediate insight into himself; they are a means by which he may know himself, and in turn understand why he acts as he does and experiences what he experiences in the light of day.

To the dreamer, the dream most often seems to be something that happened to him; an autonomous, capricious, inexplicable event he could not possibly have brought upon himself or had any part in shaping. But every dreamer has a part in what he dreams, a responsibility; dreams are not only events but *acts,* and *personal* acts, no matter how impersonal or transpersonal a meaning they might achieve. They have their source and their motivation in the energies and inertias of the inner world in much the same way that the seemingly capricious happenings of the weather have their source and "motivation" in the energies and inertias of nature. We endure the weather, having no choice; we seem to have to endure our dreams. Certainly they are as far beyond our *rational* control as are hurricanes and rain and sunny days; nevertheless, we in our individuality make them.[28]

It is impossible to imagine that the forces of the natural world should ever simply cease working; that rivers and seas and winds should stop, seeds not fall, fruits not grow, no matter how barren the landscape. Dreams are less mysterious if we remember that the forces of the inner world are as incessantly active, and that it is through dreams that we as individuals most directly perceive the qualities of their effects upon us and our effects upon them.

A dream seems to be two things at once: an act, event, experience, *and* the sensory organ by which that act, event, experience is perceived. We are conscious of the mechanisms of sensory perception as regards the physical universe; no such mechanisms, as far as we know, exist to serve us in the immaterial inner world. But in dreams we see, hear, smell, taste and touch, often with a clarity and immediacy we never experience in our perceptions of other events. *What* we perceive are aspects of reality not generally accessible by any other means. They are brought to our consciousness, forced into it, by the psyche itself as it struggles toward the realization of its potential wholeness. In doing so, it makes use of a kind of organ of perception that is a composite of all the senses, yet capable of responding not to objects but to symbols. Thus in the dream perception leads directly to *apperception,* consciousness of the self. Out of the tensions, frictions and collisions of the forces of energy and inertia in the inner world, the inner eye is opened and sees, the inner ear hears, but in the immediacy of the experience the perception and the event perceived seem most mysteriously to be the same.

The dream whose meaning is confined to the moment reflects, emphasizes or illuminates the dreamer's momentary preoccupations in ways that make it easy to see that the dream itself is a personal act, something done in the inner world in response to a given situation in the outer world. Such dreams are often compensatory: if, for example, the dreamer has during the day been acutely depressed, his dream in the night may reflect the opposite, a kind of liveliness and peace which counteracts the destructiveness of the day's feelings; if he has been feeling brawny and powerful in the day's affairs, he may dream that he is puny and weak. For the psyche, it is always a question of balance and proportion. The dream's furnishings, setting and story may be worlds removed from anything the dreamer knows at the moment, but the manner of dreams is always symbolic and by virtue of this, dreams are likely to have greater scope and deeper meaning *as personal acts* than the dreamer's acts in the outer world—greater scope and deeper meaning to him, that is, since in his dream he is acting

63

entirely on his own, out of his intrinsic individuality. His identifications and his mask give him little or no security in the inner world; so he is more truly himself when he dreams.

Some dreams are concerned with the past, with what the dreamer has forgotten, rejected or repressed or with what he might never have been aware of having experienced—in short, with aspects of his personality around which certain vital energies are constellated and bound. In dreams like these, the past is not relived; it is discovered by the dreamer as *present,* a past somehow weathered by all the time since, but unchanged, the essential human energies still active in it, the essential conflicts and concerns precisely as they were—as though it were a stretch of ground he had moved away from some time ago, but now he discovers he never really left it and finds it changed by time only in the slow and subtle ways that time changes memory. These dreams happen out of no evident concern for a momentary situation, stimulated perhaps by nothing the dreamer can find in the world he has grown into. Nevertheless, they happen for a reason and it is usually discoverable beyond the limits of the immediate situation, yet subtly informing it, encompassing neither the moment nor the year but the state of being the dreamer has come to. It usually turns out to be this *state of being* that stimulates the dream and provides the yardstick according to which it is meaningful.

Some dreams spring out of regions of the inner world where light has never fallen before. They seem to have nothing to do with any present or past situation. It is as though the dreamer took a sudden step outward, beyond anything he has known or experienced, onto a stretch of ground still sodden with the dividing waters. It is his step, suddenly his ground, suddenly personal, in the deep sense that any unknown valley or forest or field becomes personal the moment we enter it for the very reason that we are there. What happens in such dreams has probably always been happening: the dreamer simply comes at last upon it. He does it out of human necessity, out of a driven need to explore the inner world.

Finally, there are transpersonal dreams, whose content is archetypal. As they happen, they may strike the dreamer as utterly alien, springing out of some reaches of the inner world as far away as the stars, having as little to do with him as an individual as sunspots and showers of meteors. But the total impact of these dreams is often the most startling experience the dreamer may have, and often such dreams are the most meaningful to him, for they spring out of that region of himself where he is directly related with Being.

But in spite of the above discussion, dreams cannot be readily classified or placed in categories according to type or meaning. The dream always deals in symbols, and it is the very nature of the symbol to refer intensively and extensively at the same time, to connote infinitely more in its statement about an immediate situation, since it directs the finite toward the universal or brings the universal to bear upon the finite. The range, therefore, is always vast, no matter how specific and minor a point is being made. And whatever the materials of the dream might be, its meaning is the strict concern of the dreamer, for the dream is a private act and a responsible act only within the limits of privacy. It may deal in universals but not at all in the same way that science and art deal in universals. Works of science and art are public acts and therefore publicly responsible; if they are to endure, they must achieve a "degree of credibility"—as Bertrand Russell puts it—that most of mankind can accept. The degree of credibility is the crux of the problem of dream interpretation. Only the dreamer can say whether, and to what degree, a particular interpretation is credible or not. This is true even of those dreams whose contents seem to be transpersonal; the dream is his and it is meant to inform him in his individuality; it is only as he acts on the basis of the dream that the effects of the transpersonal may be felt by his fellow men. So it is the very privacy of the dream and the impossibility of isolating it from the dreamer and from his unique situation that rule out any scientific classification of dreams and any single, universally applicable, method of interpretation. It should be obvious, also, that "dream books" and any kind of "objective" dictionary of dream symbols are the last things that would be of any use.

The dreams that follow are not presented as universally valid nor as models of this or that "kind" of dream. They are quoted as the patients recorded them and are included here because they may be helpful in clarifying much of this discussion about the dream as a phenomenon and much of the earlier discussion about those natural modes of action of the psyche that we call identification, the persona, and so on. It is necessary to remember that the dreams occurred while the patients were active in the psychotherapeutic situation and that the interpretations that accompany them are fragmentary, the whole meaning having been arrived at within the situation and having been of no concern to anyone but the dreamer and the therapist. It is also important to remember that this "whole meaning" is arrived at through more than the mere telling and listening and thinking thereafter; the process involves all those subtleties of inflection, gesture, hesitation and silence that are vital parts of human communication.

One of my patients was a young woman who worked as a clerk in a post office. She was twenty-eight years old and normally intelligent, but she looked and acted like a shy girl of seventeen. She was acutely distressed in her personal relationships and in her dealings with the world generally. A weakling of a father and a power-obsessed mother made life at home chaotic for her. She dreamed:

"I am about to go swimming with a group of people. A lifeguard tells me that a fog is approaching and that we should take shelter. We see a huge black veil moving across the sea, and we all run to a little hut where we close, lock and bar all the doors and windows."

The dream continues:

"Two people are found dead in a room. A special investigator goes to find out the cause of the deaths. He is also found dead. No one can understand how these deaths have occurred. A second special investigator sees someone else being killed just after a small cut is made over the person's neck. Then little spurts of blood appear on the furniture and rapidly progress right around the room. A chameleon slowly appears; they mark his trail as he moves around the wall."

The two parts of the dream are complementary. The first reveals her desire and need to enter life by going "swimming with a group of people," but the moment she attempts to do so, the fog comes and she has to run for shelter. Anxiety works in the dream, providing the "lifeguard" to warn her and the hut to shelter her. She knew she was not ready to enter life, but she did not know why. Here the question of *why?* is asked, and in the second part it is answered.

The special investigator who is inexplicably killed symbolized an early attempt at psychotherapy that had failed. The second investigator symbolized at once the new psychotherapeutic situation and her own *inner resolution,* the prerequisite if healing and growth are to take place. Given both here, she experienced in the symbol of the chameleon her fatally quick willingness to take on the shades and shadows of her surroundings, to identify herself with her chaotic background, and thus to kill, to keep in a room full of death, her own individuality. Blameful though her parents might have been, her problem, as the dream insists, was that she accept her distinction from them and her responsibility for herself and her fate.

Another of my patients, who was a successful and respectable banker, found life meaningless, full of anxiety, guilt and depression. This was not hard to explain: in relying entirely on success and respectability, he had betrayed himself. He dreamed:

"I am in a room with a cardsharper, a blond tough type. Downstairs is the bar of a pub. I had seen some unpleasant reference in a newspaper about the dishonesty of the place; I am therefore on my guard. The game he shows me is a variation of the three-card trick, but it is played with bills and invoices. He gives me money to bet with. I make up my mind not to risk any of my own money.

"Presently a monster of evil walks into the room, dressed like a doctor and carrying a doctor's bag. He is so evil that I take to my heels and run. The front door is open. I seemed to have left it so. I dash out, not daring to grab my overcoat, and try to get around the first corner of the street without detection. I awake as from a nightmare."

Later, in discussing the dream, the patient added that the corner seemed to be in the town where he was born and that the "doctor" seemed a caricature of one of his father's partners.

This is one of those unsettling dreams with which we are all familiar: everything is the opposite of what we know and expect of ourselves; everything is irrational, "unnatural." It was certainly unnatural for the banker to be in such a place, consorting with such characters, meeting such a monster of evil. The dream is the opposite of his persona and of everything he had identified himself with, and that is its point. He knew nothing about those aspects of his own nature which we call the shadow—but this is rather like living in a country where wild beasts roam and refusing to acknowledge the danger and the good they might do if tamed. The monster of evil is an "archetype" of great power and authority, as full of energy as the grandest beast, a part of life and as such neither good nor evil. Only the dreamer's ignorance could make him see this essential part of himself as "evil." Throughout the dream he remains sensible: careful not to bet any of his own money, playing the game on his own terms with bills and invoices, and quick to run at the sight of the monster. He had even left the door open. And in his comments about the dream he related it to the past, seeing the "archetype" as a caricature. What he should have done, what he had to accept to do was to act, in his terms, foolishly and irrationally; to stand his ground, take a good look and see that the "monster" was a "doctor" and that, therefore, his energy was available in the cause of health.

In the inner world as in the outer, energy is energy and power is power; it is always a question of the uses we choose to make of them.

A patient who was a pious orthodox Jew, secure in his knowledge of sacred lore and in what he took to be his "religion," dreamed:

"I kept two poisonous snakes as pets. There was a strong subjective feeling which is difficult to describe in words. I did not find these snakes attractive pets and was not attached to them as I would have been attached to, perhaps, a dog. Later on, I was reciting my prayers, in particular the Amidah [the most intimate and solemn prayer of the Jews], which I usually say at the window of the drawing room facing east. On this occasion I was standing at the bookcase at the opposite end of the window and facing west. Instead of having my tallith [the prayer shawl] around my neck, I had the two snakes. Members of my family were present and on finishing the prayers I took the snakes from my neck and fed each one an outsize asparagus stick. I do not remember where these sticks came from. I was watching them eat them and was looking at one in particular, which caught my eye and looked at me; whereupon it attacked me and bit me in the neck. Its bite being fatal, I died in the dream, simultaneously waking up."

The patient lived without loving and tried to compensate himself for this fatal lack by his orthodoxy and his piety. His religion was all intellect (the bookshelf); knowledge without love had turned him westward, toward the kingdom of death. The dream is direct and emphatic: his lovelessness emerged as an onanistic attitude toward life; when he prayed he had the poisonous snakes, not the tallith, around his neck. It is better to know nothing at all of piety and religion and never to pray than to know and pray without love.

A Protestant minister dreamed:

"There is an old lye pit that has been carelessly abandoned. It was used to consume things that should have been liturgically destroyed. This lack of care has let consumptive forces get into all the stones of the church.

"A prayer room with big ropes in it. When people gave their gifts, they tied a knot in the rope as an act of worship, and as a sign that they had given. I didn't feel it was an accurate bookkeeping method. Told they were stored in cellar when all tied, and new ropes put in their places."

The dreamer was not concerned about whether tying knots in a rope was a proper way of worshiping; he was only worried that it was not a good way of keeping accounts. Yet he had counted on the church to destroy "liturgically" his own evil. The lye pit has been carelessly abandoned, liturgical destruction is impossible, so the very stones of the church have become "consumptive" to him. Again, it is knowledge without love, prayer with the lips and the intellect, a matter of bookkeeping; there is no commitment. In this case it is very serious, since the dreamer was a minister, an acting man of God.

Another patient dreamed that a great net had been passed over the heavens and brought all the saints down to earth. The moment they touched the earth, they were transformed into animals.

All these patients had one thing in common (and they have it in common with most of their fellow men): they would not face and accept the shadow. When they dreamed these dreams, they forced themselves, as it were, to look at what had leaped out of the darkness of their being, and took a step in the direction of self-knowledge.

A woman dreamed:

"I had gone to see a woman friend of my husband's who had moved (back?) into a larger house than before in a row of wooden houses with yards at their backs. One tree in her backyard, she took me to see, which she had been watering and which was doing well.

"In a field I noticed somewhat to the right a little group of trees with a path around them that made a ring. I thought it was a lovely sight. Perhaps it was an English landscape. How had the path come about? Perhaps by sheep walking in a circle. . . ."

The image of the circle around the group of trees is a *mandala,* projected in an elementary and, one might say, primal form. In Eastern religious tradition, the mandala is a symbol of wholeness; the great medieval rose window is a Western equivalent. Occurring everywhere and in many variations, it is a public symbol, but in this dream it occurs privately as a direct expression of the inner world of the dreamer. Had the patient drawn or painted such a mandala, as so many patients in the psychotherapeutic situation do, it would have had to be taken simply as a statement of hope and aspiration. But here, in the privacy of the dream, it is an aspect of inner reality, an expression of the archetype Self. And again, as in the dream about the "word" and the "animal," the significance of the natural order within the psyche is emphasized. The "animal" had perhaps made the circle around the trees, the "lovely sight."

A dream is an act, an event, an experience, and in so being it is as little accessible to pure reason as such acts, events, experiences in the outer world. We may try to understand and to interpret, holding as much as we can to the logical and reasonable, but in the long run what we hope for is a degree of credibility. For the patient in the psychotherapeutic situation the degrees of credibility his dreams in their meaning may achieve depend upon the extent to which he is open in his summation of himself and in his relations with the therapist. Openness is very hard to achieve. Theoretically, it should be easier to be open with the therapist than with oneself, for he neither judges, moralizes nor condemns; certainly it is infinitely harder to be one's own judge, discover one's own morality, condemn and forgive oneself in independence.

But if the psychotherapist does not judge, moralize, condemn or instruct, what does he do other than listen to dreams and try to interpret them; listen to indulgent self-confessions and complaints and say a word of comfort?

70

He participates in a human relationship. We are, in a sense, each other; our inner worlds are, in effect, the same. Just as we, as individuals, go together across the same fields and seas, through the same cities, across the same mountains and through the same forests, deserts and swamps, so we go in the inner world, as individuals, across the same landscapes. Only in this sense is the "brotherhood of man" a meaningful phrase. We grow in the one world as we grow in the other, urged toward a state of health and well-being which in both worlds depends upon balance, harmony and wholeness. Science has taught us a great deal about the conditions of bodily growth and health, about the obstacles to be met and overcome and how to sustain ourselves in sound biological ways. But do we know—specifically, does the psychotherapist know—the course and conditions of growth and health of the psyche? In other words, is there a reliable natural history of man's progress through the inner world, a sound pattern of growth from the state of genesis, when there was nothing but something nebulous, to the state of wholeness and the experience of the psyche as a totality in and of itself?

I believe that there is and that it is to be found in the Bible—from Genesis, when God said, "Let there be light," to Golgotha and the Resurrection.

*These are the secret words which the Living Jesus
spoke and Didymos Judas Thomas wrote:*

And he said:
Whoever finds the explanation of these words will
not taste death. Jesus said:
Let him who seeks, not cease seeking until he
finds, and when he finds, he will
be troubled, and when he has been troubled, he will
marvel and he will
reign over the All. Jesus said: If
those who lead you say to you:
"See, the Kingdom is in heaven,"
then the birds of the heaven will precede you.
If they say to you: "It is in the sea,"
then the fish will precede you.
But the Kingdom is within you and
it is without you. If you (will)
know yourselves, then you will be known
and you will know that you are
the sons of the Living Father. But if
you do not know yourselves, then you
are in poverty and you
are poverty.

The Gospel according to Thomas. Coptic Text established and
translated by A. Guillaumont, Henri-Charles Puech, Gilles Quispel,
Walter Till, and Yassah 'Abd al Masīh; E. J. Brill, Leidęn, and Harper
& Brothers, New York, 1959, page 3.

Figure 5. Man's emergence from the Beast

Figure 6. The artist's signature

PART TWO

Genesis

In the beginning God created the heaven and the earth.

And the earth was without form, and void; and darkness was upon the face of the deep. And the Spirit of God moved upon the face of the waters.

POETRY ITSELF seems to begin with the question of the origin of things. The first poets we know about—Vedic, Egyptian, Babylonian and Chinese—were all compelled to ask it, to imagine the universe at the instant of creation. It must have been very difficult even then, certainly it is impossible now to stand open-eyed and imagine a time when all this did not exist. The sounding of the question forces the eyes shut, as though any possible answer at all could only come from inside, as though the question were really aimed inside. Darkness, the poets all agree, came before light; the creation myths themselves must have emerged out of personal night. The poet must have done all but the final work with his eyes shut, the question sounding in his inner world until in his own light images arose in answer. Such images depended not at all upon cool observation of the world around him, but only upon the warmth of his own imagination searching his own darkness. It came to be a question of his own origins as well and of his own becoming.

75

No matter where or when they lived when the question sounded, or by what kind of people and scene they were surrounded, all those poets who lived before the time of the writing of the Book of Genesis saw rising out of the dark images in answer that were remarkably alike.

Chaos in simultaneity was what they saw. Past the instant when infinite nothingness becomes something, when heaven is separated from earth or the cosmic egg breaks or the primeval sweet-water ocean mingles with the primeval salt-water ocean, or the original incomprehensible One shakes itself and becomes the understandable first Two, the gods leap forth and the universe teems with life. Man himself does not yet exist, except in so far as the gods represent him, each deity standing for some aspect of his infinitely various nature—for his virtues and vices, ideals, desires, lusts, primal urges, all autonomous (as in fact they seem to be autonomous to each of us in our beginnings), all existing in a state of near or total war. Then the gods, for various reasons of discontent or ambition, or for no good reason at all, decide on the creation of man.

A badly damaged tablet exists from the First Babylonian Dynasty, that tells how the goddess Mami, urged by Enki and other deities, created man from clay mixed with the blood of a slain god.

> Let them slay a god,
> And let the gods . . .
> With his flesh and his blood
> Let Ninhursag (Mami) mix clay.
> God and Man
> . . . united (?) in the clay.[29]

From the ruins of the city of Ashur, there is a tablet dating back to approximately 800 B.C. which gives another version:

When heaven had been separated from the earth, the trusty twin,
(And) the mother of the goddesses had been brought into being;
When the earth had been brought forth (and) the earth had been fashioned;

When the destinies of heaven and earth had been
fixed; . . .
The Great Gods
(And) the Anunnaki, the great Gods,
Seated themselves in the exalted sanctuary
And recounted among themselves what had been cre-
ated. . . .
What (else) shall we do?
What (else) shall we create? . . .
In Uzumua, the bond of heaven and earth,
Let us slay (two) Lama gods.
With their blood let us create mankind.[30]

The aboriginal poets of pre-Aryan India thought not of a god
or gods at the beginning of things but of a First Man, Purusha
(later, Prajapati, and later still, Brahma). He was

a personification of the all-containing life-matter and
life-force itself, yearning to develop into teeming
worlds. And he was impelled to create by a two-fold
principle. On the one hand he felt lonely, destitute and
fearful, and so brought forth the universe to surround
himself with company; but on the other hand he also
felt a longing to let his substance overflow, wherefore he
said to himself: "May I give increase; may I bring forth
creatures. [My italics]"[31]

It would be hard to improve upon this deeply personal de-
scription of a very familiar state of mind and heart.
The ancient Chinese also imagined a cosmic man named
P'an Ku (*P'an,* "shell of an egg," *Ku,* "to secure, to make solid").
He was the offspring of the original dual powers, the Yin and
Yang, and they set him the task of giving form to chaos and of
making the heavens and the earth. In this task he is closely related
to Ymer of Scandinavian mythology.

> It was Time's morning,
> When Ymer lived
> There was no sand, no sea
> Nor cooling billows;
> Earth there was none,

No lofty Heaven;
No spot of green;
Only a deep profound.[32]

One of the ancient poets wrote:

If you wish to know the origin of Yüanshih [an avatar of P'an Ku], you must pass beyond the confines of Heaven and earth, because he lives beyond the limits of the worlds. You must ascend and ascend until you reach the sphere of *nothingness* and of *being,* in the plains of the luminous shadows. [My italics][33]

Like Ymer, P'an Ku in dying gave birth to the material universe. His head was changed into mountains, his breath into winds and clouds, and his voice into thunder; his left eye became the sun, his right eye the moon.[34]

From Ymer's flesh the earth was created
From his bones the mountains
From the skull of the ice-cold giant the Sky
From his blood the surge.[35]

This theme of death and creation—of dying in order to give birth—is sounded and explored again and again by the ancient poets. Purusha, to relieve his loneliness and fear and to let his substance overflow, was sacrificed, presumably to himself, by the gods who were apparently his children.

Purusha has a thousand heads, a thousand eyes, and a thousand feet. On every side enveloping the earth, he transcended it by a space of ten fingers.

Purusha himself is this whole, whatever has been, and whatever shall be. He is also the lord of immortality, since through food he expands.

Such is his greatness; and Purusha is superior to this. All existing things are a quarter of him, and that which is immortal is three quarters of him.

With three quarters, Purusha mounted upwards. A quarter of him again was produced here below. He then became diffused everywhere among things animate and inanimate. . . .

When the gods, performing their sacrifice, bound Purusha as a victim, there were seven pieces of wood laid for him round the fire, and thrice seven pieces of fuel employed.

With sacrifice the gods worshiped the sacrifice. These were the first institutions. These great beings attained to the heaven where the gods, the ancient Sadhyas, reside.

When they divided Purusha, into how many parts did they distribute him? What was his mouth? What were his arms? What were called his thighs and feet? The Brahman was his mouth. . . . The moon was produced from his soul; the sun from his eye. . . . From his navel came the atmosphere; from his head arose the sky; from his feet came the earth; from his ear the four quarters; so they formed the worlds.[36]

Whether the poets see the origin of things in terms of first man or life force or whatever, the gods come in a multitude immediately after the instant of creation. These gods proceed to the creation of man out of common stuff and some of their own essence. We have always imagined that the gods created us; but, except in the Book of Genesis, it was they who partook of our nature, and so they remained multitudinous, a chaotic crowd with no reliable scheme of precedence among them, maintaining chaos. From the *Rg Veda* and the Babylonian *Enuma Elish* to Hesiod, there are evident the poets' efforts to refine and individualize the crowded pantheons. No matter how orderly the natural world came to be seen to be, the inner world remained chaotic, and the best the poet could do was to hold onto his sense of this simultaneity. There was no possibility of resolving the duality of the human fact: the dust mingled with the blood of the gods; the one soul split in two and, owing to that original division, shattered into uncountable fragments; the one body split, and each part was doomed to seek but never truly find its mate. No matter how deeply or with what richness of imagination men probed the world inside themselves, they all came—except in the Book of Genesis—to hover over the tragic chasm, the divine in their natures on one side, the brute on the other, and had no choice but to be blown this way and that in the violent crosscurrents.

Yet in the *Rg Veda* there is a hymn with a question that haunts each phrase as a refrain: "Whom, then, shall we honor with our oblations?"

Vedic theologians were greatly puzzled by this until they decided there was a god, Ka (*who*), and that it was he who was being honored in the hymn.[37] But clearly the refrain is the original question directed at chaos itself, out of the poet's dissatisfaction with the fragmentary and multitudinous; the ontogenetic principle, the urge of the psyche toward the One and Whole, was already at work.

There is also the "Hymn of Creation," one of the oldest surviving statements of doubt. It is doubt of a serene kind; the poet is not buffeted in the chasm, but settled somewhere, holding still in the midst of the mystery:

Then even nothingness was not, nor existence.
There was no air then, not the heavens beyond it.
What covered it? Where was it? In whose keeping?
Was there then cosmic water, in depths unfathomed?

Then there was neither death nor immortality,
Nor was there then the torch of night and day.
The One breathed windlessly and self-sustaining.
There was that One then, and there was no other.

At first there was only darkness wrapped in darkness.
All this was only unillumined water.
The one which came to be, enclosed in nothing,
arose at last born of the power of heat.

In the beginning desire descended on it—
That was the primal seed, born of the mind.
The sages who have searched their hearts with wisdom
know that which is is kin to that which is not.

And they have stretched their cord across the void,
and know what was above, and what below.

Seminal powers made fertile mighty forces.
Below was strength, and over it was impulse.

But, after all, who knows and who can say
whence it all came, and how creation happened?
The gods themselves are later than creation,
so who knows truly whence it has arisen?

Whence all creation had its origin,
he, whether he fashioned it or whether he did not,
he who surveys it all from highest heaven,
he knows—or maybe even he does not know.[38]

The Book of Genesis is distinguished from all that comes before it and all that comes after by the fact that the original question is answered in a new way. For the first time there is only one creator and maintainer of man's world, one God Who created and Who transcends all cosmic matter, a spirit who summoned all things into being by the mere utterance of their names. Man remains dust, but it is dust taken up and shaped in the image of the one God. In the sudden realization of the unity of God, there arises the possibility of the unity of man. There is an end to chaos, except as man himself chooses to make it.

> And the Lord God formed man of the dust of the
> ground, and breathed into his nostrils the breath of life;
> and man became a living soul.
> And the Lord God planted a garden eastward in
> Eden; and there he put the man whom he had formed.
>
> Genesis, 2:7–8[39]

When He breathed the breath of life into the man He had formed, the Lord God of Genesis created the inner world as He had created the outer: the man became "a living soul." The dust is pagan, as old as time and inescapable, but here no blood is required for the mixing, there is no sacrifice except of a breath. Out of the One everything proceeds; and everything is maintained, the inner world and the outer, in the light of His awareness.

The revelation that both the inner and the outer orders of experience have a common source, partake of the nature of that source and are even one with it made possible the further growth of the psyche, for this revelation insists upon the wholeness of man. Man's growth toward wholeness—the ontogenesis of the psyche in the midst of, perhaps through the blessing of, all the dualities and oppositions of human existence—is the transcendent theme explored by the poets of the Bible. The poetic spirit seems to have been seized by this revelation and to have surrendered to it. For hundreds of years hundreds of poets waited and watched, and out of their silence they sang with wonderful clarity about what they saw as the light flashed farther and farther inward and simultaneously outward onto all that was unimagined and unimaginable before. Man suddenly speaks directly to his God, his God answers—and that series of dialogues begins that sounds mightily above all the tumult of history and passion recorded by the Bible. How is the individual related with the world? with his fellow men? with himself? How, above all, is he related with Being? The answer to the last question becomes the answer to all the others, and it is contained in the initial revelation.

In the Old Testament, the great theme is developed primarily through dialogues between God and man. Man stands his ground and hears God's voice out of the whirlwind and sees Him manifest Himself in the world of nature with lightning and earthquakes and pillars of fire. But the theme is brought to its awesome fulfillment in the New Testament, where the psyche is wholly at one with the creator and maintainer of all things and the kingdom of God is known to be within.

The waters divided, the earth set in place, the dust shaped as Adam, and Adam placed in the garden, the drama of man's progress toward wholeness, of the psyche's ontogenesis, begins.

The garden was no paradise, unless one thinks of infancy as paradise. There is nothing in the early verses of Genesis that implies an ideal *human* condition, an original state of wholeness, self-contained, self-sustaining, idyllic. There is no "dreaming innocence" except insofar as lack of consciousness may be considered innocence. During the first days in the garden there was an ignorance of violence and brutality, and this might confirm us in thinking it idyllic; but the violence and brutality were there and were quickly discovered. The poets of *Genesis* do not describe a "lost paradise" but step by step, in symbolic terms, they render the growth of human awareness. Eden is the "garden" of infancy.

Adam was put into the garden to till it and look after it, and there the Lord God spoke to him:

> . . . of every tree of the garden thou mayest freely eat:
>
> But of the tree of the knowledge of good and evil, thou shalt not eat of it: for in the day that thou eatest thereof thou shalt surely die.
>
> Genesis 2:16–17

Here the Lord God speaks for the first time since He brought the world into being by the utterance of the Word. He turns from His outward creation to the task of shaping man's inner world, and witn the first words addressed directly to him He separates him on the instant from all the rest that He has made. He hands down the first of His laws, and the thunder of it has been ringing in our ears ever since. We have heard it as the primal curse and the primal blessing: curse, because it is aimed at the psyche's primordial inertia; blessing, because as we hear it infancy ends and we are stirred to meaningful action. In being given the law, Adam was given the gift of choice, a gift denied to all other living things.

> And the Lord God said, It is not good that the man should be alone; I will make him an help meet for him.
>
> And out of the ground the Lord God formed every beast of the field, and every fowl of the air; and brought them unto Adam to see what he would call them: and whatsoever Adam called every living creature, that was the name thereof.
>
> Genesis 2:18–19

This act of *naming* is the first step out of mindlessness; the power to differentiate is the first sign of the growth of consciousness. It prepares the way for the creation of Eve, the *truly other*.

> And the Lord God caused a deep sleep to fall upon Adam, and he slept: and he took one of his ribs, and closed up the flesh instead thereof;
>
> And the rib, which the Lord God had taken from man, made he a woman, and brought her unto the man.
>
> And Adam said, This is now bone of my bones, and flesh of my flesh: . . .

> And they were both naked, the man and his wife,
> and were not ashamed.
>
> Genesis 2:21–23, 25

In the inner world in the beginning there is no distinction between male and female; the waters are mingled, the principles so interlocked and intertwined as to seem, not whole, but simply one and the same. They must be differentiated, experienced in their distinction as principles of being, if there is to be action between them, and creativity. This would seem to imply that the psyche is whole in the beginning, suffers division and then must struggle to regain its original perfection, a process that is, on the face of it, the old pagan round. But the critical factor here is human individuality. The Lord God addressed Adam as *human,* gave him the law and the gift of choice even before He called upon him to name the animals. In its ontogenesis the psyche struggles toward *wholeness in individuality;* and in the beginning individuality is simply a potential, a gift. In the creation of Eve, the poets symbolize the separation of the male and female principles within the inner world, the first step in making the potential actual; they hold to the truth of human existence and the facts of daily life. The consciousness of the separation does not come at once: Adam and Eve remain one ("bone of my bones and flesh of my flesh"), naked and unashamed, and he does not see her as truly other until they take the next necessary step, choose to break the law and find themselves to be separate.

> And the eyes of them both were opened, and they
> knew that they were naked; . . .
>
> Genesis 3:7

As the creation of the inner world proceeds, as the psyche develops, there is an invariable pattern of action: the Word is uttered, the ear hears, the choice is made, the eye opens, and what stands revealed is a new aspect of human reality. This archetypal pattern appears here for the first time, in what has always been called the Fall of Man. It is, I suggest, the opposite, for it makes creativity possible in *both* orders of experience. Without the awareness of the truly other, nothing could have or can happen. Taken as the poets' symbol of an aspect of reality in both orders of experience, the breaking of the law (and its conse-

84

quences) becomes a moment of revelation. With the act of choice, the human element enters; the inner world, like the outer, is found to be a world of duality, a world of opposites in constant interplay. From the psychologist's point of view, it is now that, so to speak, the stone that has blocked the springs of creativity begins to be rolled back.

The breaking of the law is significant on another level: merely to differentiate, to *name*, is not enough. The next necessary step is toward discrimination, the fruit of the experience of what is named, which we call a sense of values.

> . . . Behold, the man is become as one of us, to know good and evil: and now, lest he put forth his hand, and take also of the tree of life, and eat, and live forever!*

> Genesis 3:22

Full awareness of the world's nature is God's prerogative, but that Adam and Eve threatened it by knowing good from evil is not the reason they were driven out of the garden. The reason seems to be that, by virtue of their knowledge, they might go farther, eat of the tree of life and live forever. The tree of life had always been there and the law did not apply to it—until now. Apparently, lacking the crucial knowledge, Adam and Eve might safely have eaten of it and lived forever in some kind of mindless immortality. But the principle at work in them chose for them a different course ("It was the serpent," Eve said, "that misled me, and so I ate it."): with the eating of the apple, human reality is established and violence begins. The Lord God cursed Eve with pain and said to Adam: "in the sweat of thy face shalt thou eat bread."

At the same time, the growth of awareness of values brings to view a new symbol, which is no longer the paradise of mindless infancy but the Tree of *Life*. The way toward the realization of the vision of the tree of life does not lead backward into an unconscious, inert mere "reaching out one's hand," but points creatively forward into the perplexities of life. The immature psyche experiences the primal urge toward growth and thus toward creativity as a curse, as the life force is felt to be aimed directly against inertia, and creating anxieties, becomes a spur to the awakening mind.

* See Part III, p. 231.

Hence, the Cherubims with the "flaming sword . . . to keep the way of the tree of life" were significantly stationed by the poets "at the east of the garden," a symbol for sunlike, dawning awareness. A legend says that the way to this tree had been blocked before by the tree of knowledge of good and evil which grew around it as an impenetrable hedge.[40]

"*Therefore* the Lord God sent him forth from the Garden of Eden, to *till* the ground from whence he was taken." (Genesis 3:23) The Hebrew word used here stems from *abad* and is usually translated "to till"; etymologically, it connotes to do service, to labor, to work. In perfect simplicity the human condition in both the inner and outer orders of experience is depicted here. The poets, using as a symbol a most direct and immediate everyday experience of agriculturalists, state—at this decisive point of the unfolding of the drama of the psyche's growth toward wholeness—*the theme* which in ever renewed variations resounds throughout the Bible as the *opus magnum* of man: *to cultivate* not only the soil, but *the very substance of his mind.* [My italics]

It is this crucial insight that makes the Bible the common treasure and sacred book of millions of people. The tools of understanding that the modern science of depth psychology has given to us not only reveal the Bible's inexhaustable abundance of deepest wisdom, but the tools themselves seem to have been fashioned by its essential truth.

And a river went out of Eden to water the garden; and from thence it was parted, and became into four heads.

Genesis 2:10

According to the legend, this river flows from beneath the tree of life and provides the water "that irrigates the whole earth." The garden begins to emerge as "paradise" in a new and deeper sense: it is the poets' symbol, not of lost innocence, but of potential wholeness. The drama of man's progress toward wholeness and the drama of the psyche's growth begin in the midst of this symbol as a *scene,* but now the action moves out of it. As Adam and Eve are driven out and the gates shut behind them, the garden as a symbol rises as a kind of scenic backdrop against which the rest of the drama will be played. From this new perspective, it becomes a vivid image of man's potential wholeness.

Figure 7. *The Tree of Life*

Cain and Abel

THE EXPULSION from the garden leads directly to an encounter with the problem of action and individual responsibility. The symbol of wholeness recedes into the distance and the dualities and oppositions of human experience rule the scene. Out of the knowledge of separateness of the male and female principles comes a deeper knowledge, which the poets symbolize in Adam's sons.

Cain and Abel were opposites: Abel, the shepherd; Cain, like Adam, a tiller of the soil. Brothers doomed by their natures to war against each other are a common achetypal motif: as symbols they have many levels of meaning, all of which are focused in man's experience of the perpetual and seemingly inevitable conflict between the "good" and the "bad" in both his worlds.

> And in process of time it came to pass, that Cain brought of the fruit of the ground an offering unto the Lord.
>
> And Abel, he also brought of the firstlings of his flock and of the fat thereof. And the Lord had respect unto Abel and to his offering:
>
> But unto Cain and to his offering he had not respect. And Cain was very wroth, and his countenance fell.
>
> And the Lord said unto Cain, Why art thou wroth? and why is thy countenance fallen?
>
> If thou doest well, shalt thou not be accepted? and if thou doest not well, *sin* lieth at the door. And unto thee shall be his desire, and thou shalt rule over him. [My italics]
>
> Genesis 4:3–7

The question asked here is direct and unequivocal: which part of human nature is the acceptable one? Which is cherished by the Lord, which rejected? What part of human nature must be sacrificed—*made sacred?* The word *sin* is used for the first time in Genesis, and it heralds the first act of human violence in Biblical tradition.

> And Cain talked with Abel his brother: and it came to pass, when they were in the field, that Cain rose up against Abel his brother, and slew him.
>
> Genesis, 4:8

When they emerged from the garden (the symbol of wholeness), Adam and Eve—having chosen, so to speak, to choose—brought with them the problem of good and evil, and it is immediately exemplified in action by their sons. What emerges from the symbol of duality (the warring brothers) is the evil part, the brutal and violent portion. Cain looms as a vital figure against the vision of the garden and in vital relation with it: in him, the symbol of the psyche's potential wholeness begins to be infused with meaning. Since the encounter with Cain and what he represents of inner reality is a vital, inescapable step in the development of the individual, the first "murder" becomes a most meaningful act if it is taken as symbolic of *inner* experience. Here the poets of Genesis, being wholly at one with their theme, are led to save the brutal and unredeemed in human nature, the better to explore the possibilities of the individual's relation with it and its eventual redemption.

> And the Lord said unto Cain, Where is Abel thy brother? And he said, I know not: Am I my brother's keeper?
>
> And he said, What has thou done? the voice of thy brother's blood crieth unto me from the ground.
>
> And now art thou cursed from the earth, which hath opened her mouth to receive thy brother's blood from thy hand;
>
> When thou tillest the ground, it shall not henceforth yield unto thee her strength; a fugitive and a vagabond shalt thou be in the earth.
>
> Genesis 4:9–12

In the legends, Abel is imagined to grow in good and Cain in wickedness; additional motives are found to explain their enmity and the murder, and it is said that "the ground changed and deteriorated at the very moment of Abel's violent end." It is also said that Cain, having asked the crucial question, "Am I my brother's keeper?" went further:

> Thou art He who holdest watch over all creatures, and yet Thou demandest account of me! True, I slew him, but Thou didst create the evil inclination in me. Thou guardest all things; why, then, didst Thou permit me to slay him? Thou didst Thyself slay him, for hadst Thou looked with favorable countenance toward my offering as toward his, I had had no reason for envying him, and I had not slain him.[41]

At Colonus, Oedipus said:

> I suffered those deeds more than I acted them. . . .
> I had been wronged, I retaliated; even if I had known what I was doing, was that evil? Then knowing nothing, I went on. Went on. But those who wronged me knew, and ruined me.[42]

For Cain as for Oedipus, it is a question of the source of motive—of action, therefore, and of ultimate responsibility. The further growth and development of the human psyche hinges upon the answer; the very *existence* of the *human,* distinct from but in relation with the forces of nature, is at stake. It is very significant that the Greek hero went blind to his doom, while Cain, though cursed, was given a sign for his protection. Both were blind to the fact of their responsibility: within the inner world, the dark, brutal, violent element is always irresponsible, is driven, and clings to irresponsibility. Oedipus and Cain are perfect symbols of man's experience of the inner world at this stage of its development. But the poets of Genesis see farther than the poets of Greece in imagining that the Lord God "set a mark upon Cain, lest any finding him should kill him" (according to the legend, "God inscribed one letter of His Holy Name upon his forehead"). Oedipus remains brutal in the sense that the animal is brutal, blindly driven by the autonomous forces of nature, and he dies without having had an insight into the possibility of another way. The mark on Cain's forehead preserves him, as a symbol, for the further exploration of the theme until its culmination in the awareness of man's unique prerogative: his ability—by virtue of the developing personality and within a limited freedom—to choose.

Cain went east of Eden to the land of Nod, took a wife, bore children, and built a city. Adam's seed was renewed in Seth and first comes to flower in Noah.

> And God saw that the wickedness of man was great in the earth, and that every imagination of the thoughts of his heart was only evil continually.
>
> And it repented the Lord that he had made man on the earth, and it grieved him at his heart.
>
> And the Lord said, I will destroy man whom I have created from the face of the earth; both man, and beast, and the creeping thing, and the fowls of the air; for it repenteth me that I have made them.
>
> Genesis 6:5–7

Having posed the crucial question of the source of motive and action and of responsibility in the symbolic struggle of the two brothers; having preserved the evil one whose influence would seem to have spread through all creation—the poets seem now to identify themselves with his brutality and set aside what their insights have implied as to the possibility of meaning in human existence. With the Great Flood, they now take their symbolism from what may have been an historical event—bring down darkness, and destroy under the waters the multitude of men, leaving nothing of life but what is in the ark. In this way they dramatize the psyche's persistent urge to retreat, to return to the primal state when the waters were not yet divided. They do not avoid the issue: when the waters subside and life and consciousness are restored, the scene is set for the confrontation of two fundamental problems of human nature. Both are central to the theme.

> And Noah began to be an husbandman, and he planted a vineyard:
>
> And he drank of the wine, and was drunken; and he was uncovered within his tent.
>
> And Ham, the father of Canaan, saw the nakedness of his father, and told his two brethren without.
>
> And Shem and Japeth took a garment, and laid it

upon both their shoulders, and went backward, and covered the nakedness of their father; and their faces were backward, and they saw not their father's nakedness.

And Noah awoke from his wine, and knew what his younger son had done unto him.

And he said, Cursed be Canaan; a servant of servants shall he be unto his brethren.

Genesis 9:20–25

According to the legends, during the time in the ark, only Ham, the dog and the raven broke Noah's law imposing continence on all the inhabitants, and Ham's punishment was that his descendants were "men of dark-hued skin."* They say also that it was Canaan, Ham's son whom Noah cursed, who called his father's attention to the spectacle inside the tent. The earliest interpretations in both rabbinical and patristic literature see the incident as an attempt by Ham to castrate his father.

In his drunken condition Noah betook himself to the tent of his wife. His son Ham saw him there, and he told his brothers what he had noticed, and said, "The first man had but two sons, and one slew the other; this man Noah has three sons, yet he desires to beget a fourth besides." Nor did Ham rest satisfied with these disrespectful words against his father. He added to his sin of irreverence the still greater outrage of attempting to perform an operation upon his father designed to prevent procreation.[44]

Ham's story contains the essence of the problem that occupied the Greek poets; under the name of "Oedipus complex" it has served as a foundation for a great part of modern psychology and seems to have been proven to have scientific importance. That the essence of it (and of the "Electra complex") is to be found in the Bible, a book whose power and influence have been felt for two

* For the psychologist, it is very interesting that segregationists find religious justification for their position in this symbolic event. They project unconscious guilt onto a scapegoat and call it "the will of God."[43]

thousand years by millions of people, has been overlooked or ignored.

> What is today the heritage of the individual was once a new acquisition and has been handed on from one to another of a long series of generations. Thus the Oedipus complex too may have had stages of development, and the study of prehistory may enable us to trace them out. Investigation suggests that life in the human family took a quite different form in those remote days from that with which we are now familiar. And this idea is supported by findings based on observations of contemporary primitive races. If the prehistoric and ethnological material on this subject is worked over psychoanalytically, we arrive at an unexpectedly precise result: namely that God the Father once walked upon earth in bodily form and exercised his sovereignty as chieftain of the primal human horde until his sons united to slay him. It emerges further that this crime of liberation and the reactions to it had as their result the appearance of the first social ties, the basic moral restrictions and the oldest form of religion, totemism. But the later religions too have the same content, and on the one hand they are concerned with obliterating the traces of that crime or with expiating it by bringing forward other solutions of the struggle between father and sons, while on the other hand they cannot avoid repeating once more the elimination of the father. . . .[45]

This statement by Freud appears in a paper entitled "Psychoanalysis and Religious Origins."

The Book of Genesis proves that the Oedipus complex did have "stages of development," moving toward resolution of the problem; it also proves that later religions *can* avoid repeating the "elimination of the father." Ham's story does not fit the "scientific" scheme because the father is not killed. The poets approach the "crime of liberation" with new insight: they deal with it a number of times in Genesis, and they resolve it at last in the *Akedah,* on a level of awareness never approached by the pagan poets. There is no patricide; no traces of the crime are to be obliterated; there is no expiation and no repetition.

The essence of the Electra complex (in psychoanalytic terminology, the daughter's unconscious tendency to be attached to the father and hostile to the mother) is found in Genesis in the story of Lot's daughters.

> Then the Lord rained upon Sodom and upon Gomorrah brimstone and fire from the Lord out of heaven;
>
> And he overthrew those cities, and all the plain, and all the inhabitants of the cities, and that which grew upon the ground.
>
> Genesis 19:24–25

The symbol is again that of the brutality and destructiveness of nature. When Lot's wife looked back on it, she turned into a pillar of salt.

> And Lot went up out of Zoar, and dwelt in the mountain, and his two daughters with him; for he feared to dwell in Zoar: and he dwelt in a cave, he and his two daughters.
>
> And the firstborn said unto the younger, Our father is old, and there is not a man in the earth to come in unto us after the manner of all the earth:
>
> Come, let us make our father drink wine, and we will lie with him, that we may preserve the seed of our father.
>
> And they made their father drink wine that night: and the firstborn went in, and lay with her father; and he perceived not when she lay down, nor when she arose.
>
> And it came to pass on the morrow, that the firstborn said unto the younger, Behold, I lay yesternight with my father: let us make him drink wine this night also; and go thou in, and lie with him, that we may preserve the seed of our father.
>
> And they made their father drink wine that night also; and the younger arose, and lay with him; and he perceived not when she lay down, nor when she arose.
>
> Genesis 19:30–35

As in Ham's story, the immediate meaning of the action is conveyed in terms of sexuality. On this level, Ham's concern is simply to prevail as the source of the seed, and the concern of Lot's daughters is simply that human life continue. According to Jewish commentary,

> Lot's daughters believed that the entire world, together with all the inhabitants, were destroyed, and the continuation of the human race depended upon them; they therefore decided to bear children to their father.

Origen, the great Christian commentator of the third century A.D., was moved to discuss the incident at length:

> After this is reported that very famous story in which it is written that his daughters stole by deception intercourse with their father. I do not know if anyone can so excuse Lot in this as to hold him innocent of sin. Nor again do I think that he can be accused of being guilty of such serious incest. For I do not find that he beguiled or took by force his daughters' virginity, but that he suffered deceit and was craftily overcome. But again, he would not have been beguiled by his daughters, unless it were possible to make him drunk. Therefore, he seems to me to have been partly at fault, partly blameless. For he can be excused for he is innocent of the charge of concupiscence and lust and because he neither wanted it nor even consented to their wills. But he incurs guilt because he was able to be deceived because he drank too much wine, and this not once, but twice. For Scripture seems to be satisfied on this point, saying, "For he was unaware of it when he lay with them and when he rose up."
>
> Concerning his daughters, this cannot be said, for they deceived their father with laborious trickery. But he was so overcome with wine as not to know that he slept with his elder and with his younger daughter. See what drunkenness does! See how great a crime intemperance leads to. See and beware, you against whom this evil is not an accusation, but a habit. Drunkenness deceived whom Sodom did not deceive. He burned with

woman-fires whom the flame of sulphur did not singe. Lot was deceived by craft, not willingly. Therefore he is in the middle between the sinners and the just.

But I think the case of his daughters is worthy of more careful consideration, for perhaps they do not merit as much blame as is thought. For Scripture reports that they said to one another: "Our father is aged, and there is no one on earth who might lie with us, as it is fitting for all the earth. Come, and let us ply our father with wine, and let us sleep with him, and let us force semen from our father."

As far as those things which Scripture says of them, it seems to be satisfactory. For it appears that Lot had told his daughters something of the imminent consummation of the world through fire, but, as the girls had not learned everything completely, they did not know that, with the region around Sodom destroyed by fire, there remained yet much unharmed space in the world. They had heard that at the end of the age the world and all its elements would be baked in the fiery flame. They saw the fire, they saw the sulphury flames, they saw everything being devastated.

They saw too that their mother had not been saved; they suspected that something had occurred as had happened in the time of Noe and that they, with their Father, were alone preserved to repair the posterity of the race. They therefore felt a desire to restore the human race and thought that the beginning of the restoration of the age was to come of them. And however large might seem the charge against them of having stolen intercourse with their father, still larger would have been the impiety of, as they thought, destroying the hope of any human posterity by preserving their chastity. Therefore, on account of this reasoning they acted, I think, less guiltily than hopefully and reasonably. They softened and loosened their father's sadness and rigor with wine. They entered on separate nights and separately conceived of the unwitting man. They did not repeat or seek intercourse again. Where in this situation is the crime of lust, whence the charge of incest? How can that be called vice which is not repeated in the doing? I am afraid to say what I think—I am afraid, I say, that the incest of these girls was chaster than the purity of many other women. Let married women strike themselves and ask whether they approach their husbands for this purpose alone—to beget children—and whether, after conception, they desist.[47]

Saint Ehpraem of Syria, a Doctor of the Church in the fourth century A.D., wrote:

Since the daughters were afraid to live in a devastated city in the mountains and believing that all creation was consumed in a flood of fire, like Noah's generation in a flood of water, [they committed incest].

The girls pretended saying, "We are afraid to sleep because of visions. Our mother comes like a statue of salt and stands before us. And we see Sodomites burning. We hear the voices of women crying amidst the flames, and little children consumed with fire appear to us, therefore do not sleep, for our tranquillity. Take the wine and let the night gleam with vigils and be preserved from terror." After they saw his senses overcome with wine, and a deep sleep suffusing his limbs, the elder daughter entered and stole semen from the sleeping, unfeeling inseminator. The next day she led in her sister that she too might be a wife for an instant, and a widow for eternity. Then after their conceptions were noticeable, the younger strongly berated her elder sister saying, "It would have been better for us to be sterile than to die shamefully and for us to remain with our father without sons than that our father should be alone without daughters. What excuse will we make at the hour of judgement; what response will we give at the time he will kill us? Girls, he will say, who I have said did not know men at Sodom, who has known you here on the mountain? Will we say that the wind caused us to conceive? And when the time of bearing is upon us, what shall we do?"

97

While they were hesitating, Lot called them and said, "For some time I have been secretly regarding your bellies and day by day you confirm my suspicion against you of adultery. Tell me whence you have conceived and when and where and by whom were you seduced?" The elder daughter said to her father in answer: "Our husbands urged our mother to conceal it from you and show us to them. For although nature made us spouses of them, your lack of sons made us their sisters. But they approached us like brothers and when for some reason our mother had to leave, they rose against us and applied force like tyrants. As soon as mother returned and saw us, she threw them quickly out of the house. But our heart took consolation in that they were our spouses, not lechers. The semen we received is from our own inseminators, even though we suffered force.[48]

"In the cave of Adullam," Jewish legend says, "Lot's daughters found the wine with which they made their father drunk. God caused the wine to be put in that place in order that they should succeed in their plan."[49]

Origen maintains that the wine came from the fruit of the wine that was an offshoot of the tree of knowledge.[50] Thus, both Jewish and Christian commentators see in the incident another level of meaning. Once the stories of Oedipus and of Electra, of Ham and of Lot's daughters are viewed from the point of view of the inner order of experience, where the commentators imagine divine intervention, they may be seen as dramatizations of a crucial phase of psychic development. The overt sexual acts—the incest, the violence of murder and castration—become symbolic of the conflict and collision of the forces of the inner world: the incest a perfect image of that condition of inertia that results when the individual is *identified* with his own sources as the parent—mother or father—represents them; the "crime" against the parent the perfect image, then, of the urge to independence, to the realization of individuality and creativity in oneself and of one's own accord. Identification with the parents is inevitable and natural in the early stages of the psyche's development; liberation from that state of identification is also natural and is experienced in the inner world as "violent." The "crime" is necessary but not, as the poets of Genesis make clear, necessarily a crime. The pagan poets could not see any escape from the guilt of it; in Genesis there is no guilt. Ham's act is rude and violent, a brutal attempt that fails, and his children incur the father's curse. This curse seems to be a further intensification and deepening of the meaning of the incident; liberation from the parental image can only be accomplished as an *inner* act; Ham proved his ignorance of this by attempting it in the phenomenal world, and it is because of that ignorance that the father wields power in him and will continue to wield it in his children. Lot's daughters are very different from Ham: they choose to set aside Lot's identity as father, choose to see themselves not as daughters but as women first, and free themselves from the past for the sake of the future. And they are very different from their mother: she seems to have left herself in Sodom, she had fled only in her outward shape, could not help but look back, and at that instant her very shape was changed into a semblance of the chaos already wrought.

The stories of Ham and Lot's daughters, of Oedipus and Electra are archetypal; they are renderings, in symbols taken from the world of outward action, of inner experiences common to all men. It is not surprising, therefore, that they should occur in both pagan and Biblical context; what is surprising and very regrettable is that modern man has ignored the Bible's new insight, the radically different perspective from which it views this complex of experience. Yet it is the only perspective from which the sexual and criminal aspects of the stories can be seen to have any meaning in the human situation. What is necessary to psychic growth cannot be a crime, though (as in the cases of Oedipus and Electra) the necessity may lead to crime. By virtue of their new insight into the nature of man and into the true sources of motive and action, the poets of Genesis were able to see the human alternative.

They never cease to pursue the *human,* to explore the possibilities of individuality and choice in the midst of the "instinctual," the "brutal," the "driven"; they explore the possibilities of breaking within the psyche the eternal pagan rounds.

The instant Lot's wife, looking back on Sodom, turns into a

pillar of salt, the scene and the action shift radically, and there is a very meaningful change in the point of view:

> And Abraham gat up early in the morning to the place where he stood before the Lord:
> And he looked toward Sodom and Gomorrah, and toward all the land of the plain, and beheld, and, lo, the smoke of the country went up as the smoke of a furnace.
> Genesis 19:27–28

There has been a great deal of destruction and brutality: murder, the Great Flood, castration, the wickedness of the cities of the plain, brimstone and fire, and incest. The inner world has been examined in its primal state. But there has been, meanwhile, a significant counterpoint.

Abraham was Lot's uncle. Not long before he looked down on the smoke of Sodom, the Lord God had appeared to him and had said:

> . . . Sarah thy wife shall have a son. And Sarah heard it in the tent door, which was behind him.
> Now Abraham and Sarah were old and well stricken in age; and it ceased to be with Sarah after the manner of women.
> Therefore Sarah laughed within herself, saying, After I am waxed old shall I have pleasure, my lord being old also?
> And the Lord said unto Abraham, wherefore did Sarah laugh, saying, Shall I of a surety bear a child, which am old?
> Is any thing too hard for the Lord? At the time appointed I will return unto thee, according to the time of life, and Sarah shall have a son.
> Then Sarah denied, saying, I laughed not; for she was afraid. And he said, Nay; but thou didst laugh.
> Genesis 18:10–15

The annunciation "thy wife shall have a son" sounds with beautiful clarity in the midst of the destruction and brutality of the natural order. But its very *unnaturalness*—addressed as it is to the old Abraham and the old Sarah for whom things have ceased to be the way they are for male and female—seems to announce something new in both orders of experience. In the midst of the general darkness, man's relation with Being is reasserted; the human seed is, as it were, planted again in the inner world, and it will grow with greater power and greater promise than it has had before. The power and the promise are concentrated in Abraham and in his son Isaac, and it is in the drama of the father and the son that the poets of Genesis fully confront and resolve their initial theme.

The Akedah

And it came to pass after these things, that God did *tempt* Abraham, and said unto him, Abraham: and he said, Behold, here I am.

And he said, Take now thy son, thine only son Isaac, whom thou lovest, and get thee into the land of Moriah; and offer him there for a burnt offering upon one of the mountains which I will tell thee of.

And Abraham rose up early in the morning, and saddled his ass, and took two of his young men with him, and Isaac his son, and clave the wood for the burnt offering, and rose up, and went unto the place of which God had told him.

Then on the third day Abraham lifted up his eyes, and saw the place afar off.

And Abraham said unto his young men, Abide ye here with the ass; and I and the lad will go yonder and worship, and come again to you.

And Abraham took the wood of the burnt offering, and laid it upon Isaac his son; and he took the fire in his hand, and a knife; and they went both of them together.

And Isaac spake unto Abraham his father, and said, My father: and he said, Here am I, my son. And he said, Behold the fire and the wood: but where is the lamb for a burnt offering?

And Abraham said, My Son, *God will provide himself a lamb for a burnt offering:* so they went both of them together.

And they came to the place which God had told him of; and Abraham built an altar there, and laid the wood in order, and bound Isaac his son, and laid him on the altar upon the wood.

And Abraham stretched forth his hand, and took the knife to slay his son.

And the angel of the Lord called unto him out of heaven, and said, Abraham, Abraham: and he said, Here am I.

And he said, Lay not thine hand upon the lad, neither do thou anything unto him: for now I know that thou fearest God, seeing thou has not withheld thy son, thine only son from me.

And Abraham lifted up his eyes, and looked, and behold behind him a ram caught in a thicket by his horns: and Abraham went and took the ram, and offered him up for a burnt offering in the stead of his son.

And Abraham called the name of that place Jehovah-jireh: as it is said to this day, *In the mount of the Lord it shall be seen.*

Genesis 22:1–14*

This is the *Akedah* (from the Hebrew *akad,* to bind). It is read in the synagogue on the first day of the New Year and the shofar (the ram's horn) is blown on that day as well as on the Day of Atonement. The passage is read in the Anglican service on Good Friday and in the Roman Catholic service on Holy Saturday. It is also one of the central events in the religion of Islam.

Brief as the *Akedah* is, sparsely worded, with almost no hint of the feelings that must have accompanied it, it is nevertheless one of the profoundest events in the ontogenesis of the psyche and in the history of man's progress toward the realization of what it is to be a man. Readers, commentators, scholars, artists and saints have

* My italics throughout this passage.

known and felt this profundity for two thousand years. The sense has always been that with the binding of Isaac something new came into the world of human experience and that it marked ". . . a turning of the mind which divided the history of the world into two parts, one before and one after the Akedah."[51]

Its immediate background is infanticide, the ritual murder by which our primitive ancestors hoped to deal magically with the dark, feared, unknown powers of decay and death. To destroy the child was, in effect, to stop time in its passage, to wipe out the visible proof of advancing age, and so to ward off death and delay the future. It is a very old action, a very old impulse. Chronos killed his children to remove from his sight the living proof of his age. Apsu, in the *Enuma Elish,* would have liked to do the same:

> "Their way has become painful to me (says Apsu),
> By day I cannot rest, by night I cannot sleep;
> I will destroy (them) and put an end to their way,
> That silence be established, and then let us sleep!"
> *Enuma Elish,* Tablet I, 37–40*

When he exposed the infant Oedipus on the mountain, Laius was obeying the same impulse; the oracle's voice was his own. The impulse obeyed by Agamemnon in sacrificing Iphigenia was more complex, more "civilized," so to speak, more modern.

To see the *Akedah,* as some commentators have, as a protest against infanticide is to ignore what really happens in it. It is a sacred rite demanded, as Abraham felt, by God Himself. *God did tempt Abraham to the deed, but at the instant of the sacrifice it is God Himself who thwarts His own purpose.* It is this crucial paradoxical insight that makes the *Akedah* a *revelation* and Abraham the spiritual progenitor of Western man.

Necessity, the very lack of any choice in the matter and of any power to choose, is always the justification for brutality and violence. Agamemnon sacrificed Iphigenia in the name of political necessity, placating by murder a power outside himself, called a goddess. He might have chosen a different course, but by the time he came to Aulis the *idea* of war was invested with brutal powers not to be thwarted.

* *Enuma Elish,* the great Babylonian creation myth, is discussed at length in Part III, in direct relation to the case of Joan.

> He dared the deed,
> Slaying his child to help a war. . . .
> And all her prayers—cries of Father, Father,
> Her maiden life,
> These they held as nothing,
> The savage warriors, battle-mad.[52]

The *idea*—social necessity, economic necessity, religious necessity, and so on—no matter how benevolent its ends, is, more often than not, brutal in its means, the very brutality being considered necessary and just because it is committed in the dim glow of some future "good."

At the beginning of the *Akedah,* Abraham is at least in one way like Agamemnon. Though he suffered, Agamemnon did not doubt nor question Calchas, the Seer, through whom the gods had spoken, and neither did Abraham question the inner voice that demanded the monstrous act. He simply obeyed. But there is a signal difference: Agamemnon needed Calchas to tell him the will of the gods and his own fate; no such intermediary between him and his God was acceptable to Abraham, he would accept nothing but intimacy with Him. For Agamemnon such intimacy would have been inconceivable. His pantheon was created out of the fragmented psyche and was a true image of it. His gods and goddesses were symbols of human attributes, and to be favored by one of them was necessarily to incur the enmity of another, perhaps to be driven by him to ruin. It is the same within the psyche when a portion of its gifts is idolized and the rest neglected—when, in short, (whether the times are pagan or otherwise) the gods are made in the image of men. In such a situation, responsibility always rests outside; for Agamemnon, it lay with the gods. He could sacrifice Iphigenia and remain guiltless in his own eyes. According to the poets, his act made the Trojan War possible and led to his own murder and Clytemnestra's, and to Orestes's madness—violence spawning violence out of the psyche's dire fragmentation. Aeschylus, in the *Oresteia,* could see no way out of the real problem except to deny, in effect, its existence by referring it backward into a time when, as far as the human psyche is concerned, it did not exist. At the climax of the trilogy, in *The Eumenides,* both Apollo and Athena insist upon the primal state of the psyche, when the waters were not yet divided, when there was no insight into the dualities of existence, no question of the sources of motive and action and no touch possible therefore, at any point, upon the pulse of tragedy.

Apollo speaks:

I will tell you, and I will answer correctly. Watch.
The mother is no parent of that which is called
her child, but only nurse of the new-planted seed
that grows. The parent is he who mounts. A stranger she
preserves a stranger's seed, if no god interfere.
I will show you proof of what I have explained. There can
be a father without any mother. There she stands,
the living witness, daughter of Olympian Zeus,
she who was never fostered in the dark of the womb
yet such a child as no goddess could bring to birth.

And Athene, at the balloting, says:

It is my task to render final judgment here.
This is a ballot for Orestes I shall cast.
There is no mother anywhere who gave me birth,
and, but for marriage, I am always for the male
with all my heart, and strongly on my father's side.
So, in a case where the wife has killed her husband, lord
of the house, her death shall not mean most to me. And if
the other votes are even, then Orestes wins.[53]

The decision is prehuman and inhuman since the motives out of which it is cast spring, as far as the inner world is concerned, out of Adam's time, before any experience of the *truly other*. Consequently, the decision has nothing to do with the brutal human facts of the *Oresteia* that brought the trial about. The decision is *social,* it reasons away the blood curse, but it does not break the pagan round. Sophocles could find no solution for Oedipus. Oedipus could answer the Sphinx's riddle with a single word, "Man!," but when the time came for him to see the full meaning of that answer in his own life, he blinded himself. But he had been blind from the beginning: he came finally to Colonus, saying, "Knowing nothing, I went on"; and he vanished into the grove of oaks sacred to the Awful Goddesses, "Queens of dread aspect," declaring his innocence. How he died was never known, for Theseus hid his eyes against the sight. Later, Antigone said:

> Alas!
> How manifold the inheritance of woe
> Drawn from the troubled fountain of our birth![54]

The Bible's answer to this woeful cry and to the Greek's tragic sense of life may be found concisely in the verses about the sour grapes. The whole passage is unfortunately not often quoted:

> Behold, the days come, saith the Lord, that I will sow the house of Israel and the house of Judah with the seed of man, *and* with the seed of beast.
>
> And it shall come to pass, that like as I have watched over them, to pluck up, and to break down, and to throw down, and to destroy, and to afflict; *so will I watch over them, to build, and to plant,* saith the Lord.
>
> *In those days they shall say no more, The fathers have eaten a sour grape, and the children's teeth are set on edge.*
>
> *But every one shall die for his own iniquity; every man that eateth the sour grape, his teeth shall be set on edge.*
>
> ... After those days, saith the Lord, *I will put my law in their inward parts, and write it in their hearts;* and will be their God, and they shall be my people.
>
> Jeremiah 31:27–30, 33*

This singular promise, spoken out of an unshakable conviction of the intimacy between God and man, resounds again and again throughout the Bible and helps to give it a transcendent place above all other sacred books. Why have we put the book away into a place of remote sanctity? We scarcely read it any longer or understand its remarkable immediacy. Some of us have turned away from its passionate concern with the individual human being to the East, to an order of wisdom that disregarded the development of the individual and sought fulfillment in self-oblit-

* My italics.

eration.* Deep as this wisdom often is, its cyclical view remains a pagan one; life and time and the psyche continue to turn back upon themselves and the eternal round is not broken but transcended by the obliteration of nirvana. But no matter where we turn, we cannot transcend the natural order; as men, we are part of it. When we, as individuals, lack any human relations with the vast energies of that order, when they turn in unending cycles back upon themselves, we always explain our motives and actions in terms of necessity, of the driven and inescapable. We project our helpless state in symbols of monsters, dragons, werewolves, all manner of things *inhuman,* outside and beyond the human creature and bound to destroy him—and they do, whether in the shape of a beast projected into the world or, as in Oedipus's case, in the shape of his own actions. In this sense, we of the modern world are, I repeat, again profoundly pagan. All our brutality is now outside and above us, hovering in the shape of bombs and missiles that might at any moment drop, and like Oedipus and Agamemnon we see ourselves at best as instruments, having no choice but to destroy or be destroyed. We are back, it would seem, where we started; it is as though the Bible had never been written, as though we had not for two thousand years had in our hands man's estimate and resolution of the central dilemma of his nature. We have slipped back to that dim state in which, having no image of what a man is or may be, men imagined that the sources of motive and action lay somewhere outside themselves and, consequently, that responsibility lay with the gods, if anywhere.

* ". . . the orthodox Vedic view of the divine life-force and its unending play [was]—obviously a vision that involves a depreciation of the individual. Any civilization so inspired would tend to overlook the unique and personalising features of the various men and women who composed it; and indeed we find that the holy wisdom of the Brahmans largely disregarded the development of the individual. Self-discovery and self-expression were never studied as the means by which one should realize oneself and prepare to make one's contribution to the world. In fact, the whole idea of the Brahman civilization was precisely the contrary. Fulfillment was sought through self-obliteration; each was all." Heinrich Zimmer, *Philosophies of India,* Bollingen Series XXVI (New York, Pantheon Books, Inc., 1951), p. 412.

Throughout the early chapters of Genesis, the poets take up and examine the central dilemma of man *as* man; they turn it like a faceted stone which has as its center a developing image of the intimacy between man and his God. Between the Creator and Adam, that intimacy seems slight; the snake could be blamed. Between the Lord God and Cain it is closer, but Cain could question his responsibility and, in the legends, he could be imagined to fix his guilt upon God. Now, with Abraham, whatever distance there was between man and his God is wiped out. The *Akedah* establishes an abiding intimacy.

As a symbolic action, it is remarkably complex, remarkably daring, and sharply double-edged. In the beginning, Abraham is still pagan. According to the Koran, the urge to kill Isaac came to him in a dream; according to Genesis, God tempted him, he heard God's voice demand the sacrifice and he did not question it. Why not? Doesn't this leave as open as ever the question of individual human responsibility? Had Abraham killed Isaac—the living proof of his age, infirmity, eventual death—would he, like Cain, have pointed to God as the source of his evil inclination? The decisive factor here is Abraham's intimacy with his God. Sarah laughed, questioned, doubted, but Isaac was born. Whatever primitive and—up to now—"natural" impulses Isaac's youth may have stirred in the old Abraham, the sight of him must have affirmed at every moment an opposite truth: Isaac came and was visibly, palpably there, *against nature* but wholly in accordance with Abraham's experience of his God. Therefore that experience was all the more to be trusted. If his God tempted him by stirring something so old and brutal in his nature, so against his human feelings for his son and, seemingly, so violently at cross-purposes with his God's own purpose in giving him his son, then he must still trust, as Agamemnon did, even to the point of risking the humanity he has achieved up to now.*

Abraham obeyed. He traveled for three days in silence in the direction the Voice had indicated to him and "on the third day Abraham lifted up his eyes and saw the place afar off."

* Doesn't this cast a significant light on the plea in the Lord's Prayer, "Lead us not into temptation"? Do we mean Him to spare us this intimacy and the responsibility we incur with awareness of His ways?

Here the pattern of the psyche's creative action (the Word, the hearing, the choice, the seeing) is opened up and another phase is added. It is the phase of silence, a period of time when time is suspended, the senses blotted out, the inner order seemingly isolated and all its energies constellated around the seed of choice; the journey itself—whether taken by Abraham toward Moriah, or by Jonah into the whale's belly, or by Christ downward into Sheol—is an inward journey across the silent wastes of being.

> . . . An evil and adulterous generation seeketh after a sign; and there shall be no sign given to it, but the sign of the prophet Jonas;
>
> For as Jonas was three days and three nights in the whale's belly; so shall the Son of man be three days and three nights in the heart of the earth.
>
> Matthew 12:39–40

Jonah fled when he heard the Voice and came into the heart of the tempest and was cast overboard and swallowed by the great fish the Lord had prepared for him:

> The waters compassed me about, *even* to the soul: the depth closed me round about, the weeds were wrapped about my head.
>
> I went down to the bottoms of the mountains; the earth with her bars was about me for ever: yet hast thou brought up my life from corruption, O Lord my God.
>
> When my soul fainted within me I remembered the Lord: and my prayer came in unto thee, into thine holy temple.
>
> They that observe lying vanities *forsake their own mercy.* [My italics]
>
> Jonah 2:5–8

The experience takes place in the inner world and plumbs that world to its depths; the journey, the casting overboard, the elected descent are symbolic of withdrawal into the inner order and during the course of it one's own mercy spares one for awareness. In poetic terms, it is a kind of dying, a leap away from the security of the known (the known always seems secure, no matter how unpleasant it may be) into the utterly unknown; a committal to the sacrifice of what we sum ourselves up to be in order to discover how far short of the total that summation has been. One must, it seems, descend silently to the primal depths. The Sign of Jonah seems to be the Sign of silence.

> I said to my soul, be still, and wait without hope
> For hope would be hope for the wrong thing; wait with-
> out love
> For love would be love of the wrong thing; there is yet
> faith
> But the faith and the love and the hope are all in the
> waiting.
> Wait without thought, for you are not ready for thought:
> So the darkness shall be the light, and the stillness the
> dancing.
>
> Whisper of running streams, and winter lightning.
> The wild thyme unseen and the wild strawberry,
> The laughter in the garden, echoed ecstasy
> Not lost, but requiring, pointing to the agony
> Of death and birth.
>
> T. S. Eliot, *East Coker*[55]

As the silence ended, as he lifted up his eyes, Abraham "saw the place afar off." At this instant the spirit lifts: there is hope and promise in the words themselves. Then Isaac asked about the sacrificial victim and Abraham, with a remarkable blend of tragic irony and profound faith, answered that God would provide Himself with His own victim. One feels from this answer that Abraham suddenly *knows* now in the depths of his being something new, of which he is not yet conscious. His own mercy, the psyche's own forgiveness, a sudden harmony of the forces of the inner world in the face of his committal, seems to have evoked the answer, and promises a deeper answer, and on the basis of the promise he has acquiesced.

The legends say that Isaac acquiesced as well:

> "Father, make haste," Isaac said to Abraham,
> "bare thine arm, and bind my hands and feet securely,

for I am a young man, but thirty-seven years of age, and thou art an old man. When I behold the slaughtering knife in thy hand, I may perchance begin to tremble at the sight and push against thee, for the desire unto life is bold."*[56]

In this moving passage Isaac is imagined to have trustfully surrendered like Abraham; he too seems to have looked up and seen the place afar off and acquiesced to the developing situation. And here as in the Biblical passage there is a revelation of a deeply human relationship between father and son. Love is a factor between them, overruling necessity in the very act of bowing to it. Love is what was lacking in Agamemnon, Clytemnestra, Electra and Orestes, Laius, Jocasta and Oedipus, but with Abraham and Isaac it becomes the primary factor, the very crux of the commitment.

And Abraham lifted up his eyes, and, behold, behind him a ram caught in the thicket, which God had created in the twilight of Sabbath eve . . . and prepared since then as a burnt offering instead of Isaac. And the ram had been running toward Abraham, when Satan caught hold of him and entangled his horns in the thicket, that he might not advance to Abraham. And Abraham, seeing this, fetched him from the thicket, and brought him upon the altar as an offering in place of his son Isaac. And Abraham sprinkled the blood of the ram upon the altar, and he exclaimed, and said, "This is instead of my son, and may this be considered as the blood of my son before the Lord."[57]

* The legends prove again here the abiding richness of the original image. It is, in fact, the image itself which continues its own development, being re-experienced, expanded, deepened by the poet according to his own time and disposition. It is not a matter of fanciful elaboration but rather that the image as archetype continues to stir the forces of the inner world to the degree that it still holds something of the truth of the human condition. The artist would be quickest to testify to this process of creativity.

God accepted the sacrifice, accounting it as though it had been Isaac, and said:

It was manifest to Me and I foreknew that thou wouldst withhold *not even thy soul* from me![58]

Abraham, in his faith and irony, proves to have been right: God does provide Himself with His own victim. Because He foresaw the *Akedah,* He prepared for it by creating the ram in the twilight of the sixth day of Creation and left him to graze under the tree of life until an angel brought him out of Eden to Mount Moriah.[59] The ram, according to the legend, is a *knowing* victim; Satan restrains him because the time is not yet ripe. It comes to its fullness when Abraham lifts the knife, and then it is as though his own brutality leaped forth, like the calf from the fire, and takes the ram's shape, and he can *see* it and see the possibility of choosing a different way. He has no reason to believe the sacrifice will be acceptable, that the blood of the ram will be taken in place of the blood of his son, but he takes the risk, the "existential leap" beyond all certainty, and in doing so poses and answers a crucial question about the nature of God and the nature of man. Taken inwardly, as a distillation in symbolic action of a discovery about the inner world, about the nature of the psyche itself, the event, the question and the answer are momentous. The psyche proves to hold *within itself* the means with which to confront and transform its own blind and brutal forces. In the lightning flash of this insight, the inner world appears radically changed.*

There is a great deal of lore about Mount Moriah. It is said that at the end of his three-day journey, when he first lifted his eyes,

[Abraham] noticed upon the mountain a pillar of fire reaching from earth to heaven, and a heavy cloud in

* In this connection, the attention of the reader is drawn to a significant difference in the two artistic representations of the Akedah in Figures 8 and 9. While Ghiberti—true to Biblical tradition—portrays the angel as using the "Word," the other artist makes the angel physically hold the knife.

Figure 8. The Akedah, *medieval biblical illumination*

Figure 9.
The Akedah, *Ghiberti, the Baptistry of San Giovanni, Florence*

which the glory of God was seen. Abraham said to Isaac: "My son, dost thou see on that mountain which we perceive at a distance that which I see upon it?" And Isaac answered, and said unto his father: "I see, and, lo, a pillar of fire and a cloud, and the glory of God seen upon the cloud." Abraham knew then that Isaac was accepted before the Lord for an offering. He asked Ishmael and Eliezer: "Do you also see that which we see upon the mountain?" They answered: "We see nothing more than like the other mountains," and Abraham knew that they were not accepted before the Lord to go with them.[60]

The place on which Abraham had erected the altar was the same whereon Adam had brought the first sacrifice, and Cain and Abel had offered their gifts to God —the same whereon Noah raised the altar to God after he left the ark.[61]

The place is also said to be the same as Golgotha. In other words, it is a region of the psyche, a sacred precinct to be arrived at by choice, through that silence that is like dying. The need to make the journey, springing out of the psyche's urge toward wholeness, is what brings so many people to psychotherapy; what makes it so difficult is that the way necessarily lies through the primitive, subrational and dark in man's nature.

"Thou shalt love the Lord thy God with *all thine heart, with all thy soul and with all thy strength.* [My italics]"[62]

All is the crucial word: it encompasses the soul's evil along with its good. In the legend, Satan's presence on Mount Moriah is as necessary as God's. Abraham enters the sacred precinct driven by what we would call the "demonic," by those forces of his inner world that deny life and would destroy it, but there is a duality, an opposition, within the demonic itself (it was his God who tempted him); in other words, he moves into a direct experience of the dualities of man's nature, and the instant he lifts the slaughtering knife, those opposites collide and out of the resounding crash comes awareness of the possibility of choice. In really seeing his own brutality, he can see his relationship with it and thus its power over him; the eternal round is broken. The war of opposites ends and the opposites are revealed as harmonious: God and Satan stand together in the sacred precinct; Abraham, the man, stands between them. Man as *man,* an individual distinct within, and vitally related with, the forces of his being, becomes an actuality. *Personality* is established.

". . . may this be considered as the blood of my son before the Lord."

Within the inner world, the human prerogative has been asserted: the intrinsic individuality takes its stand amid the forces that surround and sustain and support it or, as it sometimes seems, are bent upon destroying it. In taking the stand, in making the choice, the very nature of those forces is revealed. The answer to Abraham was immediate: his choice, the human way, is right. The sacrifice was acceptable.

The Book of Job

THE PROBLEM posed in the *Akedah* is dealt with in the Book of Job on an intensely human and personal level. The scale is that of myth, but the immediate conflict is that of a deeply individual mind and heart. From the psychological point of view, the story of Job may be seen as a remarkable poetic exposition of man's struggle to achieve personality, a sound means of relations with experience.

The immediate situation, that of an individual in a state of acute psychic depression, is rendered with clinical exactness; the terms are symbolic, taken from the outer order of experience, but they describe the collapse of personality within the inner order and an imminent threat to the individuality itself.*

Job's world, all he thought good (and in which, to that extent, he found his identity) is swept away in a series of swift, inexplicable catastrophes. It may happen just this way in the inner world and we all know it, having had depressions descend inexplicably upon us; at such times whatever we valued is suddenly valueless. The world is lost to us as Job lost his and his family, friends and goods. One's sense of identity dwindles and nothing is promised but wretchedness, boils on the skin and a sitting place in the ashes.

In his misery Job cried out:

"What is my strength, that I should hope? and what is mine end, that I should prolong my life?"   Job 6:11

And later on he says about his life:

I loathe it. . . . I would not live alway; let me alone
for my days are vanity.
What is man that thou shouldst magnify him?
Job 7:16–17

With God's permission, Satan is the instigator of all Job's woes. There is a major contention between God and Satan: what is the sense of virtue and holiness if it is kept safe behind God's hedge, ignorant of the true nature of things? Tear down the hedge, withdraw the blessing, and what will happen to virtue and holiness? Stroke by swift stroke, Satan brought Job down to a place among the ashes.

Then said his wife unto him, Dost thou still retain *thine integrity?* curse God, and die.   Job 2:9†

Job's integrity is being tried, his very integration which has as its center his idea of the nature of *his* God and of his relationship with Him.

"What?" he replied, "Shall we receive good at the

* See chapter 33, verses 19–22. Here the poets describe a severe state of depression in clinical detail and with extraordinary accuracy.
† My italics.

hand of God, and shall we not receive evil? In all this did not Job sin with his lips." Job 2:10

He never does sin with his lips by cursing *his* God, but in his despair at "receiving evil" he does curse life and the world, and it is in this that he failed to understand and was taught.

The teaching began at once with the appearance of his three friends, who are aspects of himself, voices of his own experience of conviction, belief and doubt. It is a kind of inner discourse during which the individual, in the midst of inner chaos, listens to the "knowing" past and finds it both unknowing and comfortless.

The first speaker, called Eliphaz, had experienced in a dream something of the nature of things in depth: a spirit had passed before his eyes, *"there was silence,"* and a voice had said, "Shall mortal man be more just than God? shall a man be more pure than his maker?" (Job 4:16–17)

Eliphaz goes on to speak as one who has been able to rationalize the irrational and logically to infer the meaning of dreams; it is a question for him of not aspiring too high, of being satisfied, as a man, with a man's justice and a degree of purity commensurate with a man's low estate. But the question that sounded in the silence of his dream points to the outcome of the discourse. When Eliphaz had finished, Job complained he had scared him with dreams and terrified him with visions so that now he chose death to life. His despair was invincible. Other voices, Bildad's and Zophar's, urge common sense, penitence and humility upon Job, but thy do not touch him in his despair or come near to the root of his problem.

> Have pity upon me, have pity upon me, O ye my friends; for the hand of God hath touched me.
>
> Why do ye persecute me as God, and are not satisfied with my flesh?
>
> Oh that my words were now written! oh that they were printed in a book!
>
> That they were graven with an iron pen and lead in the rock for ever!
>
> For I know that my redeemer liveth, and that he shall stand at the latter day upon the earth:

And though after my skin worms destroy this body, yet *in my flesh shall I see God:*

Whom I shall see for myself, and mine eyes shall behold, and not another; though my reins be consumed within me. [My italics]

Job 19:21–27

This famous statement of faith, quoted as often as any in the Bible, is as full of irony as Abraham's reply to Isaac that God would provide His own victim. He is brought to the realization of his faith, that "in my flesh shall I see God," but what he sees is far beyond the idea of his God upon which his life has been built.

In his justice and his purity, he has thought he knew the *ways* of God, and that they were exemplified in him and his uprightness and his prosperity. In his own eyes he has been the living proof of the unity of man within himself, with his fellow men, with the universe, and with his God. But now, in the chaos of his life, the world and man prove to be unchanged, as full as ever of violence and brutality, and life is meaningless, death preferable. The great question is how all of this can possibly be related to his idea of his God, with whom he has always been seemingly at one.

The inner discourse continues. Reason fights the extremes of existential despair but never touches its source. Job goes on cursing life: he has been a righteous man and remains so, in his own eyes, even as he curses. The climax of the discourse and its diversion toward the truth of the matter comes with the entrance of Elihu. Significantly, he is a youth, a symbol of a new view of reality that is imminent. He makes a great speech to Job:

Behold, in this thou art not just: I will answer thee, that God is greater than man.

Why dost thou strive against him? for he giveth not account of any of his matters.

For God speaketh once, yea twice, yet man perceiveth it not.

In a dream, in a vision of the night, when deep sleep falleth upon men, in slumberings upon the bed;

Then he openeth the ears of men, and sealeth their instruction,

118

That he may withdraw man from his purpose, and hide pride from man.

Job 33:12–17

Elihu affirms the natural order—the snow, the small rain, the great rain, frost and clouds. He has youth's humility before the awesome neutrality of nature. As he speaks, Job is silent. He has proclaimed his righteousness for the last time, saying, if all his claims were lies, then "Let thistles grow instead of wheat, and cockle instead of barley. The words of Job are ended." Like Abraham, he takes the sign of silence, and out of that silence Elihu speaks as though he were the voice of Job's own dawning awareness.

> Teach us what we shall say unto him; for we cannot order our speech by reason of darkness.
>
> Shall it be told him that I speak? if a man speak, surely he shall be swallowed up.
>
> And now men see not the bright light which is in the clouds: but the wind passeth, and cleanseth them.
>
> Fair weather cometh out of the north: with God is terrible majesty.
>
> Touching the Almighty, we cannot find him out: he is excellent in power, and in judgment, and in plenty of justice: he will not afflict.
>
> Men do therefore fear him: he respecteth not any that are *wise of heart*. [My italics]

Job 37:19–24

The moment Elihu is silent, God speaks directly to Job out of the whirlwind:

> Who is this that darkeneth counsel by words without knowledge?
>
> Gird up now thy loins like a man; for I will demand of thee, and answer thou me.

Job 38:2–3

As Job had earlier cursed and denied life, God now affirms it and all His creation in its multitudinous forms. The whole of His speech seems to be meant to put Job in his proper place in the midst of that creation, and this *proper place* turns out to be one far outside and beyond any considerations of righteousness. But Job's despair is not relieved, any more perhaps than one's own would be by an awesome gauging of one's stature in relation to the land-scape and the stars. In Elihu's speech, as an inner voice, Job seems to have sensed the way, to have taken the first step toward the experience of a true relation with Being, but it is only in his discourse with God that he comes to the roots of creativity, where any opposition between Essence and Existence is beside the point.

But, first, he keeps his silence:

> Behold, I am vile; what shall I answer thee? I will lay mine hand upon my mouth.
> Once have I spoken; but I will not answer: yea, twice; but I will proceed no further.
>
> Job 40:4–5

God repeats His demand that Job be a man:
"Deck thyself now with majesty and excellency; and array thyself with glory and beauty."
And adds at last:
"Then will I also confess unto thee that thine own right hand can save thee." (Job 40:10, 14)

Everything else was preliminary to this last statement. Job and God have come now to the decisive encounter. In the midst of it God confesses to man, His own creature, that it is not He but man himself who can save himself by his own right hand. It is man who must discover his own relationship with the ways of Being.

Immediately after this confession, God reveals the mode of that discovery:

> *Behold now Behemoth, which I made with thee;* he eateth grass as an ox.
> Lo now, his strength is in his loins, and his force is in the navel of his belly.
> He moveth his tail like a cedar: the sinews of his stones are wrapped together.
> His bones are as strong pieces of brass; his bones are like bars of iron.

He is the chief of the ways of God: he that made
him can make his sword to approach unto him.

Job 40:15–19*

The single isolated beast is made to stand for all the blind forces of creation, for the *natural* in the inner as well as the outer order of experience. Now, as Job's eyes meet the eyes of the beast, as it were, and as his ears hear the voice of his God, Job himself comes to stand for all men who, in their confusion about man's true nature and about the ways of God, aspire to an unnatural distinction *from* the orders of experience, an intimacy with *their* God which would in effect rule out nature.

Throughout the poem Job has insisted upon his distinctness; he asserts his individuality at every point. Never once does he call upon the spirits of his forefathers; never once does he ask his wife or his friends to save him or even to soothe his sufferings or to do anything but leave him alone to die in his misery. But it is the very source of his distinctness that is in question: his righteousness. As the discourse reaches its height just before the appearance of Elihu, Job cries out for the time in the past when his God preserved him, when he was honored and princes fell silent as he approached. "When the ear heard me, then it blessed me; and when the eye saw me, it gave witness to me," and the dying blessed him and the widow's heart sang for joy.

"I put on righteousness, and it clothed me: my judgment was a robe and a diadem." (Job 29:14)

Here, unaware, he goes to the root of his troubles. His identity has resided exclusively in his righteousness and in his God's testimony to it in the phenomenal world; his personality, his relations with himself, with his fellow men and with the world, has been founded entirely upon it. When the visible proof of his righteousness was swept out of the world; when family, friends and goods no longer exemplified his virtue; when his God no longer testified to his identity by so shaping the world as to mirror it— then he would turn away and die. He stops short of an almost magnificent *hubris*—that ultimate sin because it is the ultimate confusion—only by virtue of his unshakable belief in intimacy with his God. He sins in his belief that he *is* his own righteousness, that it

* My italics throughout the passage.

sums him up completely, and in cursing a creation that no longer testifies to that fact.

But righteousness is of small consequence when it is a matter of achieving a relation with the whole of life. The true encounter between Job and his God, between Abraham and his, between any man and his, takes place in that sacred precinct that is located beyond any considerations of right and wrong, moral and immoral, good and evil. It must happen in a "teleological suspension of the ethical"[63] out of which, and only and exclusively out of which, true value comes. But to say this makes no sense at all if it is taken to refer to the phenomenal world and human action in it. Men cannot suspend the moral and ethical in their dealings with each other without inevitable catastrophe. This decisive encounter can only happen in the inner world—paradoxically, it *must* happen there if man is ever to fulfil himself.

Confronting Behemoth, Job really confronts the unnamed stuff of life, all that will forever remain beyond the reach of righteousness; the tempestuous, brutal, violent, the mindless which man fears in himself and in the world outside because he is not mindful of it.* God tells Job to look, by *seeing* to bring this unnamed stuff of life into the light of his awareness, *to accept it as a part of himself and to achieve a human relation with it.* Behemoth is a natural inhabitant of the inner world, and though he may be beyond the reach of righteousness, he is not beyond the reach of rightness. The vast energies of Being that he symbolizes may drive man, rule him, overthrow him and destroy him as a man, or when, as a man, he experiences them rightly, they may do the opposite. Behemoth is the source of individual woe or the source of the energies of human creativity.

When Job has fully taken in Behemoth, so to speak, he comes out of his despair. The despair itself would seem to be the poets' symbol for his containment within the dark forces of his own nature, a containment which had itself seemed *natural* to him, for he had been able to rationalize and justify it on the basis of his righteousness. He insisted he was right to despair; and he *was* right, but for the wrong reasons. Through despair, one may come

* Modern translations of the Bible render *Behemoth* as "hippopotamus," etc. This does not affect the meaning of the symbol except to blur it poetically and restrict its scope of reference.

to the direct encounter and the direct involvement with one's self, one's *other* nature, and once despair has been seen for what it is, there is the possibility that it may be transformed. Despair may therefore be creative: it may seem destructive as an earthquake to everything known and valued, but it is possible that out of the abyss a new and higher knowledge and a truer value may come. And this depends on the depth of the experience. Job's despair in its very extremity brings him to his encounter with God and thus to his encounter with Behemoth, the "chief" of His ways. Struck so to the depth of his being, the true catharsis takes place for him.

Like the *Akedah,* the Book of Job emerges, in my view, as decisive in the history of man's experience of himself and of the true nature of the inner world—a landmark, as it were, in the ontogenesis of the human psyche. Here, as in the *Akedah,* the poets have recorded in a whole symbolic action the encounter of human individuality with those forces of the inner world that seem inimical to humanity and individuality and that *are* inimical up to the instant they are seen in their true light, when awareness comes and relations with them may be achieved. As symbolic actions, both stories are archetypes of man's experience of the psyche's urge toward wholeness and both reach their climaxes and resolutions in the instant when personality, as I have used the word, is established.

In the Book of Numbers there is a subtle variation on this major theme. The incident occurs during the Exodus, at a time when "the soul of the people was much discouraged because of the way."

> And the people spake against God, and against Moses, Wherefore have ye brought us up out of Egypt to die in the wilderness? for there is no bread, neither is there any water; and our soul loatheth this light bread.
>
> And the Lord sent fiery serpents among the people, and they bit the people; and much people of Israel died.
>
> Therefore the people came to Moses, and said, We have sinned, for we have spoken against the Lord, and against thee; pray unto the Lord, that he take away the

Figure 10. The Vision of the Beast

serpents from us. And Moses prayed for the people.

And the Lord said unto Moses, Make thee a fiery serpent, and set it upon a pole: and it shall come to pass, that *every one that is bitten, when he looketh upon it, shall live.* [My italics]

And Moses made a serpent of brass, and put it upon a pole, and it came to pass, that if a serpent had bitten any man, when he beheld the serpent of brass, he lived.

Numbers 21:5–9

To look at the "agent of death," really to see the image of destruction in whichever of its innumerable shapes, averts death, thwarts destruction. Under the impact of the encounter with the image itself, the psyche naturally and immediately acts to counteract it. This is a principle of action within the inner world; it is not nearly so mysterious or rare as it might at first seem.

And there appeared a great wonder in heaven; a woman clothed with the sun, and the moon under her feet, and upon her head a crown of twelve stars:

And she being with child cried, travailing in birth, and pained to be delivered.

And there appeared another wonder in heaven; and behold a great red dragon, having seven heads and ten horns, and seven crowns upon his heads.

And his tail drew the third part of the stars of heaven, and did cast them to earth: and the dragon stood before the woman which was ready to be delivered, for to devour her child as soon as it was born.

Here, in chapter twelve (verses 1–4) of the Book of Revelation, the encounter in conflict of the basic forces of the inner world is rendered by the poets on a level at once cosmic and utterly direct. The Mother, the creative principle, in the very act of creativity is at once assailed by the opposite principle, the "dragon," the destructive, the essentially inert. The ultimate archetypal principles meet headlong. Then there was war in heaven:

And the great dragon was cast out, that old ser-

125

pent, called the Devil, and Satan, which deceiveth the whole world: he was cast out into the earth, and his angels were cast out with him.

And I heard a loud voice saying in heaven, Now is come salvation, and strength, and the kingdom of our God, and the power of his Christ: . . .

Revelation 12:9–10

The beast, "that old serpent," is not killed here or in any of the other great encounters with him in the Bible. The mediaeval illuminations (Figures 10 and 11) reproduced on pages 124 and 127 show phases of the encounter and of the true meaning of it. On page 124 the people are revealed in the act of *seeing* the "inner agent of death," the winged serpent dragon with human face. Page 127 depicts the casting out of the great dragon of Revelation, but the artist has been inspired to a remarkable juxtaposition of incidents in the decorative detail with which he surrounds the scene. The enlargement of the decoration in the lower left-hand corner reveals a hunter shooting arrows against the "beast," but the arrows are turned back upon the hunter himself. (". . . and he shall

Figure 11. The Dragon expelled from Heaven

let go the goat in the wilderness." Leviticus 16:22)* The attempt to *kill* the beast kills the developing personality, for it deprives the individual of the energies of the natural order that are his as soon as he achieves a human relationship with them. The dragon of Revelation flourished on earth and never ceased to threaten "the woman which brought forth the man child." It was a later sentimental Western tradition that encouraged the idea that the "dragon"—the natural order within the psyche—might and in fact must be killed[64] (i.e., denied, repressed, eradicated) and that man might thereby escape the human predicament and human responsibility.†

The principle (the *image* and the individual's direct confrontation with it) is revealed in its most majestic and paradoxical light in the Gospel according to St. John, chapter three, verses 12–15:

> If I have told you earthly things, and ye believe not, how shall ye believe, if I tell you of heavenly things?
>
> And no man hath ascended up to heaven, but that he came down from heaven, even the Son of Man which is in heaven.
>
> *And as Moses lifted up the serpent in the wilderness, even so must the Son of Man be lifted up:*
>
> *That whosoever believeth in him should not perish, but have eternal life.*‡

* There is a variation on this theme in the Christian legend of the vision of Monte Galgano: a bull had strayed and refused to come home. His owner ordered that he be slain, but the arrows shot against him flew back against the archer and it was the archer who fell dead.

† Fortunately, there are still poets, artists, psychologists and others who know the truth of the matter. The following passage comes at the climax of a recent novel: the *head* is that of a sow, killed in an orgiastic hunt by a group of boys, but the voice is interior, heard by the "poet" among them. " 'Fancy thinking the Beast was something you could hunt and kill!' said the head. For a moment or two the forest and *all the other dimly appreciated places* echoed with the parody of laughter. 'You knew, didn't you I'm part of you? Close, close, close! I'm the reason why it's no go? Why things are what they are?' [My italics]" William Golding, *Lord of the Flies* (New York, Capricorn Books, 1955), p. 177.

‡ My italics throughout the passage.

Figure 12. The Serpent on the Cross

The extraordinary juxtapositions of this passage lead backward through all of man's insights into the problem of self-knowledge, back as far as the beginning, when humanity first asked the first questions about human nature; but they lead simultaneously forward toward a future when each individual may conceivably experience their full meaning. Again, in the illuminations reproduced in Figures 12 and 13 the medieval artists reveal the depth of their experience of the meaning of the passage. In Figure 12, the serpent is raised on the cross and Moses stands below in a gathering of dignitaries of the Christian Church; the Latin inscription on the banner refers to the original incident in the Old Testament. Figure 13 is reproduced here exactly as it is arranged on a single page of an early manuscript. The *Akedah*, the raising up of the brazen serpent, and the Crucifixion are brought together by an artist who felt their vital relation each with the other and was inspired to the creation of a whole symbol of awesome proportions.

The answers to the questions posed by the Delphic injunction, about who the knower is, what is to be known and why in the knowing the individual will be more peaceful and creative, should now be within reach. It is out of the very effort to know that the true *knower* comes into being; it is out of the very effort to establish relationships with both orders of experience that the *means* of those relations, the *personality,* is established. To the degree that this *spiritual means* expands and grows, the individual emerges in his distinction within the orders of experience and simultaneously in vivid and passionate involvement with them, the knower approaches knowledge of himself, and to the extent that he knows through experience, through the direct encounter, the dark, unnamed, mindless stuff out of which he came and which is a vital portion of his nature, he is able to lift it up into the service of his own creativity.

> And as Jesus passed by, he saw a man which was blind from his birth.
>
> And his disciples asked him, saying, Master, who did sin, this man, or his parents, that he was born blind?
>
> Jesus answered, Neither hath this man sinned, nor his parents: but that the works of God should be made manifest in him.

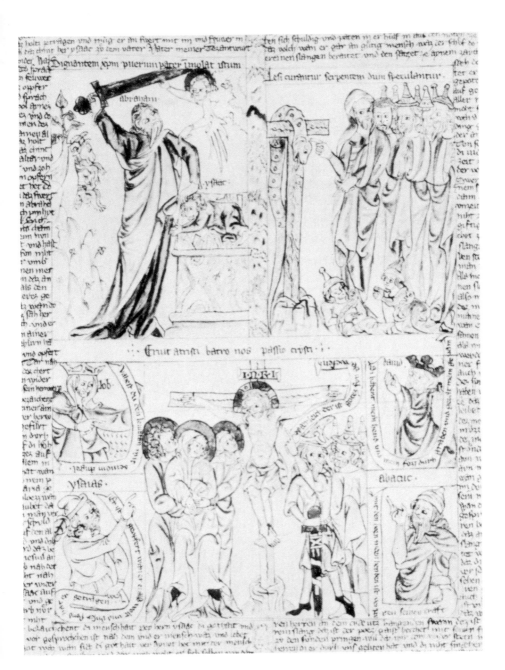

Figure 13.
The Akedah, *The Serpent on the Cross, and The Crucifixion*

I must work the works of him that sent me, while it is day: the night cometh, when no man can work.

As long as I am in the world, I am the light of the world.

When he had thus spoken, he spat on the ground, and *made clay of the spittle,* and he anointed the eyes of the blind man with the clay. [My italics]

And said unto him, Go, wash in the pool of Siloam, (which is by interpretation, Sent.*) He went his way therefore, and washed, and came seeing.

John 9:1–7

The doubting crowd, seeing him healed, drove him away; then Jesus spoke to them:

And Jesus said, For judgment I am come into this world, that they which see not might see; and that they which see might be made blind.

And some of the Pharisees which were with him heard these words, and said unto him, Are we blind also?

Jesus said unto them, If ye were blind, ye should have no sin: but now ye say, We see; therefore your sin remaineth.

John 9:39–41

At the end of his encounter with God and with Behemoth, the "chief of the ways of God," Job broke his silence:

I have heard of thee by the hearing of the ear: but *now mine eye seeth thee.* [My italics]

Wherefore I abhor myself, and repent in dust and ashes.

Job 42:5–6

Everything Job had lost was restored to him in double portion, and that would seem to be the poets' way of saying that when, within the inner world, the eye truly sees, it values doubly. The lots of his three friends who tried to reason away his despair were

* The modern version renders this: "—a name which means One who has been sent."

reduced; those voices failed and died within him. The fourth friend, the young Elihu, is not mentioned. The legends say that three men acquired the knowledge of God by themselves: Abraham, Job and Ezekiel, and that the fourth will be the Messiah.[65]

Job lived on for one hundred and forty years; "So Job died, being old, and full of days." (Job 42:17)

Earlier in this book, in reference to the myths of creation, a mysterious theme was sounded: the poets imagined that the first gods or the first man sacrificed themselves so the world and men could come into being. The Babylonian god Bel, for example,

> . . . cut off his own head and the other gods caught the flowing blood, mixed it with earth, and fashioned man out of the bloody paste; and that, they say, is why men are so wise, because their mortal clay is tempered with blood divine.[66]

The theme is struck more profoundly in the *Poetic Edda:*

> I ween that I hung on the windy tree,
>   Hung there for nights full nine;
> With the spear I was wounded, and offered I was
>   To Othin, *myself to myself,* [My italics]
> On the tree that none may ever know
>   What root beneath it runs.[67]

The cosmic "self-sacrifice" becomes meaningful when it is taken as symbolic of an event in the inner world, the experience of the act of choice. The emergent individuality takes action of itself, in its own world, according to its own laws and the laws of that world, in ways other than rational, abandoning what is known in a committal to the unknown, to the realm that never can be fully known, and it is in the act itself and in the committal that the "self-sacrifice" lies, and the "dying."

Lately a new romanticism about this most profound human experience is evident. Many people have been encouraging great expectations of the new "religious revival," finding proof of their hope in all kinds of signs, from mass conversions at mass meetings, mass immersions, mass healings meticulously televised—from all this to the broad intense interest in the religions of India, China and Japan. A great deal is being said about "ultimate concern" and about that vertiginous moment when truth is known and the very being transformed. There is certainly hope in the fact that modern men want experience of these things, but it is disturbing that the experience itself is being misunderstood and misrepresented. It is being made to seem immediately at hand, around the next corner; it is believed that if only the seeker runs hard enough and juggles existential concepts adroitly enough, he can catch it. What is being forgotten is that the "heroic encounters" as the poets render them are distillations of years of elected loneliness, often of despair, and always of the long, intense effort to perfect the will to that fine gleaming point at which, like the point of Abraham's knife, when the light catches it, something new of human reality is revealed. The Bible and all the other great poetic records of man's progress toward self-knowledge and the realization of his own humanity come to us, obviously, as the finished product, and one must be careful not to be misled. It is sobering to remember how long a time must have been spent in the discovery and the refinement.

> For as Jonas was three days and three nights in the whale's belly, so shall the Son of Man be three days and nights in the heart of the earth.

The long three days and three nights are inescapable. The psyche's "transformation" may happen in an instant, but that instant comes long after the immersion. Long after the Word is spoken, the ear begins to hear. The inertia of the inner world is natural and great and it guards itself with might. Long after the ears have heard, the emergent individuality may commit itself to that sacrifice of "myself to myself" and begin the painful process of the will's refinement that may bring it at last to the point when it is no longer *will* but *acquiescence,* and then the time is ripe for action, for the risking. But then the inertia is greatest, for it is directly threatened; it "acts" by its very presence within the natural order to limit and to confine, to hedge in righteousness, for example, and hold back the future, to thwart the development of the human, to hamper the ontogenesis of the psyche.

". . . Is it not written in your law, I said, Ye are gods?" (John 10:34) This was Christ's answer to the crowds who were stoning him. The primal inertia has never been more directly challenged, nor the risk that challenge entails more clearly defined. What is risked, what is sacrificed, is *present identity,* the partial, limited, seemingly essential and secure. Once committed to that risk, the leap once taken, after the long silence the eyes may lift to a view of the sacred precinct where God, Satan and Abraham stood together.

> "Do you see how Abraham my friend proclaims
> the *unity* of My Name in the world?" God said to the
> doubting angels the moment before Abraham lifted the
> knife. "Had I harkened to you at the time of the creation
> of the world, when ye spake, What is man, that Thou
> are mindful of him? And the son of man, that Thou
> visitest him? who would there have been to make known
> the unity of My Name in this world?"[68]

For Abraham, the experience of his own brutality was inescapable if he were ever to know the sudden inspiration that thwarted it; both are the ways of God, and none but man can know and proclaim them in their unity, which is His unity. The spirit does not prevail against Behemoth, but prevails *with* it. The death and the resurrection are necessary to proclaim the whole.

According to the legends, the *Akedah* ends with a dialogue between Abraham and his God, and in it Isaac emerges in his full significance as a part of the symbolic action. He is the image of the new in humanity, an archetype of growth and change, like the figure of the Child-Savior who appears in so many of the world's religions. It is through him, by virtue of his presence, that Abraham redeemed himself in his humanity, and it is upon him that the future comes to depend:

> "Didst thou not promise me to make my seed as
> numerous as the sands of the sea shore?"
> "Yes," God answered.
> "Through which one of my children?"
> "Through Isaac."
> "I might have reproached Thee, and said, O Lord
> of the world, yesterday didst Thou tell me, In Isaac shall
> thy seed be called, and now Thou sayest, Take thy son,
> thine only son, even Isaac, and offer him for a burnt

offering. But I refrained myself, and said nothing. Thus mayest Thou, when the children of Isaac commit trespasses and because of them fall upon evil times, be mindful of the offering of their father Isaac, and forgive their sins and deliver them from their suffering."

"Thou hast said what thou hadst to say and I will now say what I have to say. Thy children will sin before me in time to come and I will sit in judgment upon them on the New Year's Day. If they desire that I should grant them pardon, they shall blow the ram's horn on that day, and I, mindful of the ram that was substituted for Isaac as a sacrifice, will forgive them their sins.[69]

The scope and grandeur of Abraham's story, and Job's and of the Bible as a whole may tend to set them at a distance from us and make them seem far removed from the life we live and of very little application to it; yet like everything else in our poetic and artistic heritage from the time the Word was uttered and the world was made, these great personages and this book are the refined and polished record of man's discovery of himself in the midst of the orders of experience; records, therefore, of the ontogenesis of the psyche itself as the individual has experienced it and has been able to communicate that experience to us.

The inner order, like the outer, changes little: it is the *human* that makes the difference in both worlds and changes or is not changed, progresses or does not progress. The vast energies of the psyche are still directed toward the realization of wholeness and we still experience the fact and the effort in dreams that, intimate though they are, make use of private symbols remarkably like those public symbols of Biblical literature.

One of my patients, a Roman Catholic by upbringing, well-educated except that he had next to no knowledge of the Bible, dreamed once that he saw a rocky pinnacle, strangely lighted in a general darkness, and a trail leading upward, along which a heard of rams came leaping. Behind them came a tall old man in strange robes, a patriarch, and he climbed to the top of the peak and blew a loud blast on a ram's horn. The patient heard that blast, it woke him up. Surely at some time in his childhood he must have heard or read the story of Abraham and Isaac and responded to it, but he did not remember, and more than a year went by before the meaning of his dream was clear to him.

Another patient, whose troubles came from his unwillingness to accept any responsibility for himself or his own actions and whose feelings were concentrated in hatred for his brother, came finally to this decisive symbolic action: he dreamed he had murdered his brother and that, sitting at the family dinner table afterwards, he wrote on the tablecloth with a fork, "I killed my brother." The family rushed in, shouting that he was a fool, the police would come and take him away, but he shouted back that it was true: "I am guilty!"

Still another patient, whose behavior not only sexually but in most other ways could be summed up by the word *onanistic,* dreamed he was at the top of a lighthouse located inland, far from the sea. He was watching a group of people in a garden far below and he wanted to join them, but there was no way down. He had no choice but to leap. He got up all his courage and tried once, failed, tried again, failed, then, with that desperation that comes when even courage has proved to be not enough, he tried the third time and leaped out into the void of air. The lighthouse instantly telescoped and he walked calmly away on solid ground.

A young Chinese refugee, son of an eminent father, suffering from both these facts of his existence, dreamed:

"I was carrying my little niece of whom I am very fond; we were crossing a yard. The yard was very muddy, so I walked around the edge where the mud was comparatively firm. More than halfway around, I discovered a blunt instrument stuck into my niece's ankle, and I was in a panic to get back where I had come from and get first aid for the child because she might get an infection from the blunt instrument and the mud. I was in such panic that I ran straight into the middle of the yard where the mud was softest and I began to sink lower and lower and I was terrified. Then suddenly a man in the position of the Statue of Liberty rose up out of the mud; he was carrying a child and water spurted all around them like a fountain, to wash the mud off, and at the same time there was a bright sun shining instead of the gray sky that was there before."

The blast of the ram's horn that demands the sacrifice but simultaneously promises the blessing; the words on the tablecloth that in their declaration of personal guilt also declare the acceptance of personal responsibility; the risk of the leap out and down from the bleak lighthouse of self-sufficiency; the desire to save the wounded, Oedipus-like child that leads where the mud is softest, to the sinking, but immediately to the rising up, the cleansing and the sunlight: all these were events in the ontogenesis of the individual psyche, and they reaffirm man's ability to experience in his own way the events recorded with such grandeur in the Bible. The effort *to know* brought them about; the *knower,* as patient, might still have been frail and fearful, unable to grasp what had happened in his inner world, but the very *knowing,* the experience itself, has strength and courage in it.

To give the Sphinx the quick, open-eyed answer, "Man," does not mean that one knows the meaning of the question or of the answer. Oedipus withdrew into the lonely blind majesty of his innocence; an innocence as lacking in human meaning as his blindness. To be blind does not necessarily mean not to see: Oedipus had proof of that in Tiresias. With Tiresias, the lack of physical sight, of the view of the outer order of experience, is symbolic of inward seeing, and it is this that Oedipus never achieved. Blindness in the sense that Christ used it means vision of that other landscape and knowledge of that seemingly other order of things that gives the answer its truth and stabilizes the world.

Jacob and Esau

God created worlds and destroyed them — till Jacob came. The world was then completed and was no more destroyed.[70]

The great themes of the Book of Genesis are explored in all their depth and subtlety in the story of this man by the virtue of whose very existence the world was completed.

It is a personal story, full of the details of daily life— as though the poets, in the intensity and clarity of their vision, are moved now to express their insights on the level where clocks mark the time. In the harmony between the timeless and the timed, Jacob the man emerges in all his individuality.

Isaac married Rebecca and in time she was pregnant with twins:

> And the children struggled together within her; and she said, If it be so, why am I thus? And she went to enquire of the Lord.*
>
> And the Lord said unto her, Two nations are in thy womb, and two manner of people shall be separated from thy bowels; and the one people shall be stronger than the other people; and the elder shall serve the younger.†
>
> And when her days to be delivered were fulfilled, behold, there were twins in her womb.
>
> And the first came out red, all over like an hairy garment; and they called his name Esau.
>
> And after that came his brother out, and his hand took hold on Esau's heel; and his name was called Jacob: and Isaac was threescore years old when she bare them.
>
> Genesis 25:22–26

The annunciation to Rebecca is as direct and unequivocal as it was to the Virgin Mary: she is full of the world's enigma, the eternal Two, the opposites who will war against each other for dominion. But the Virgin was full of the One, in whom the enigma is seen to be resolved.

The legends say that as the two brothers quarreled in the womb Jacob said to Esau:

> "Brother Esau, there are two of us, and two worlds lie before us, a world on this side and a world on that

---

* In a modern translation, her question is rendered, "If it is to be thus, on whose side am I to be?"

† In the modern translation, this is rendered: "Two nations are in your womb, and the two peoples have been hostile ever since conception in you; The one people shall master the other, And the older shall serve the younger."

139

side. The one world is the world in which there is eating and drinking, the world of action and change; the world beyond, however, has nothing of all this. If it is thy will, take thou the world on this side and I shall keep the world beyond for myself."[71]

This terse, naive settlement of the quarrel is rich in paradox. It accepts the natural opposites of the psyche as twins, and accepts the natural conflict between inertia and creativity, the will to stasis and the will to change, on the part of both the brothers. The futility of the settlement is implicit in it: the choice cannot be made for one world, one order of experience, to the exclusion of the other. Jacob, choosing the world beyond for himself and the world this side for his brother, chooses modes of inertia for them both and, as it turns out, dooms each to the opposite of his choice.

Esau, born hairy, red all over, was clothed from the beginning for the world on this side, and he became a hunter, knew the seasons and the animals' ways, and smelled of the earth which fed him. Jacob was smooth and soft, lived in tents and spent his time studying sacred lore.

> [Jacob was] the opposite of his brother in this as in all respects. Jacob was born with the sign of the covenant on his body, a rare distinction. But Esau also bore a mark upon him at birth, the figure of a serpent, a symbol of all that is wicked and hated of God.[72]

Put most succinctly in the legends, this is man's experience of the shadow. But in this story each brother is the other's shadow!

> Seven days before the rising of the moon the spirit of gentleness prepares to do battle with Semael and his hordes on account of the waning of the moon. The hairy man [Esau] becomes embroiled with the smooth man [Jacob] over the beauty of the moon, and Michael and Gabriel join issue with the accusers. But at the end of the seventh day Gabriel weakens their power and the High Priest Michael takes Semael, who is on the side of the hairy man and who looks like a ram, and offers him as a kind of a sacrifice on the altar which is built as a penance at the beginning of each month. Then the su-

preme will is appeased, the moon grows big and full and the power of the ram [Esau] is consumed in the fire of the Almighty. At the time, however, that the moon [Jacob] is waning, the ram is born again, and again grows in strength, and so it will continue until the Last Day, when it is said, "The shining of the moon will be as the shining of the sun."[73]

In spite of the presence of the Almighty and of the reference to the *Akedah*, the point of view of this quotation is clearly pagan: the opposites rise, collide, fall back, rise again; the circle turns back upon itself forever until the Last Day. Here the sense and significance of the original image has been lost; but Jakob Boehme recovers it:

> The figure externally hath but a plain and child-like semblance; but yet it is a figure of the greatest Mysteries. For Esau betokens the first power of the naturall, created Adam, and Jacob betokens the power of the *other Adam, Christ;* thus doth the spirit here play with the figure.[74]

The spirit plays with the figure to great purpose. Adam's name is derived from the Hebrew *adom*, red—the red of the earth out of which he was shaped; it is symbolic of the first principle of man's nature, the principle of his origins and of his situation in the phenomenal world. As such, the rights of the "first-born" are inherent in it and the right to the blessing. Esau, beloved by his father Isaac, perfectly stands for this principle from the beginning; he is the "natural" man and has the rights to the outer order of experience and the blessing of it. Jacob, beloved of Rebecca, has neither rights nor blessing but must gain them if he is ever to move out of his tent into the world. Both brothers, taken as symbols of aspects of inner reality, seem, therefore, to reveal the psyche in its original condition: Esau representing the seeming "wholeness" of the natural order, Jacob representing the *intrinsic individuality* which must experience that order in all its ways if any real human wholeness is to be achieved. The poets of Genesis here reveal an insight of enormous significance: the essentially human, the individual, begins with neither "rights" nor "blessings"; they must be won, and won in the fields of reality.

141

And Jacob sod pottage: and Esau came from the field, and he was faint:

And Esau said to Jacob, Feed me, I pray thee, with *that same red pottage;* for I am faint; therefore was his name called *Edom.*

And Jacob said, Sell me this day thy birthright.

And Esau said, Behold, I am at the point to die: and what profit shall this birthright do to me?

And Jacob said, Swear to me this day; and he sware unto him: and he sold his birthright unto Jacob.

Genesis 25:29–33*

The Hebrew word for pottage used here is *haadam,* literally the red fruitful earth. Jacob seems to have been about to practice an ancient homeopathic magic based on the principle of *similia similibus curantur:* he was going to eat what, as a man, he lacked, and thus he would assimilate it and make it part of himself. But here, as in the story of the Golden Calf, it is primitive magic only at the start. Magic involves manipulation of the natural order to some finite purpose; when Jacob buys his brother's birthright[75] with the stuff he himself expected to eat, the purpose is changed and the magical act is moved out of the material world into the world of the psyche. The seed of truth in the magic rite is thus planted in the only ground where it may thrive and flower. The quality of the act itself is changed and the lentil pottage, the adamic fruit of the earth, becomes equivalent to the *prima materia* out of which the old philosophers attempted to distil the "philosophers' stone," the symbol of unification. Assimilation—transformation—unification: this process, as it is experienced in reality is the problem for both Jacob and Esau, and it governs their lives as human characters throughout this very human story.

The reader can now see how subtly the themes of the Book of Genesis are developed and with what grace of vision. Cain and Abel, the brothers at war against each other, in a sense stand midway between Adam—and the original insight into the dualities and oppositions of experience—and Jacob and Esau—who are also brothers at war, but they are a refined symbol; the process of refinement has resulted in the virtual elimination of brutality

* My italics throughout the passage.

and violence from the human scene. Again, the situation between them is paradoxical, but on a much deeper level. The drama of Cain and Abel was, so to speak, played against, and in the presence of the Lord God, to Whom Abel's sacrifice was acceptable and Cain's was not. With Jacob and Esau, the position is significantly reversed: Esau, like Cain, who is the "natural" man, is the favored one; Jacob like Abel, the human, gentle one, starts with nothing, as it were, but himself and his relation to his brother. Everything turns upon this natural relation, for, though Jacob does not know it (nor do we know it, within ourselves, as we start), it is through his "brother" that he has his roots in the order of things, and it is only after he has performed the ritual of winning the birthright and the other ritual of winning the blessing that he has his first experience of the ways of God.

On this level, Jacob's magic act becomes an archetype of individual experience of the inner world, a model—if we understand it rightly—for our own development. For himself, he cooks what perfectly corresponds with his brother's nature. The cooking seems to invoke his brother's presence, and he appears, famished, thinking he will die of hunger. Within the psyche, the shadow, the dark, brutal, violent, *is* famished; it hungers for the light of the human and demands it, as Cain was imagined to demand acceptance and recognition by the Lord God. So there is reciprocity even here, in the original conflict; there is a paradoxical yielding of each to the other in the name of a higher goal envisioned by neither. Jacob knows his twin well enough to be able to strike the bargain with him. Just so, the same bargain may be struck within the psyche, according to its laws, its necessity for harmony and balance, and according to one's own mercy.

When Isaac was old and blind, Rebecca heard him call out to Esau.

> And Rebekah spake unto Jacob her son, saying, Behold, I heard thy father speak unto Esau thy brother, saying,
>
> Bring me venison and make me savoury meat, that I may eat, and bless thee before the Lord before my death.
>
> Now therefore, my son, obey my voice according to that which I command thee.

Go now to the flock, and fetch me from thence two good kids of the goats; and I will make them savoury meat for thy father, such as he loveth:

And thou shalt bring it to thy father, that he may eat, and that he may bless thee before his death.

And Jacob said to Rebekah his mother, Behold, Esau my brother is a hairy man, and I am a smooth man:

My father peradventure will feel me, and I shall seem to him as a deceiver; and I shall bring a curse upon me, and not a blessing.

And his mother said unto him, *Upon me be thy curse* [my italics], my son: only obey my voice, and go fetch me them.

And he went, and fetched, and brought them to his mother: and his mother made savoury meat such as his father loved.

And Rebekah took goodly raiment of her eldest son Esau, which were with her in the house, and put them upon Jacob her younger son.

And she put the skins of the kids of the goats upon his hands, and upon the smooth of his neck:

. . . .

And Jacob went near unto Isaac his father; and he felt him, and said, The voice is Jacob's voice, but the hands are the hands of Esau.

And he discerned him not, because his hands were hairy, as his brother Esau's hands: so he blessed him.

Genesis 27:6–16, 22–23

If we take the incident as referring to the inner order of experience, the emergent human individuality is here seen by the poets in direct relation with the forces of the ancestral past, the Father and Mother archetypes, and something of considerable importance takes place. It is the mother, Rebecca, who plays the radical benevolent role. She stands in marked contrast to Tiamat, Jocasta, Clytemnestra and all the other pagan images of the destructive, inert mother principle. She had asked, "Wherefore do I live?" She gives her answer by choosing against herself and the inertia of her motherhood in order to guide her son into the guilty act that will take him into life and the fulfillment of his destiny.

According to the legends, Rebecca said, "When Adam was cursed, the malediction fell upon his mother, the earth; and so shall I, thy mother, bear the imprecation if thy father curses thee." Then she led Jacob to his father's door, and said, "Thus far I was obliged to go with thee, but now may thy Maker assist thee!"[76]

She is like Eve tempting Adam to the necessary act. Isaac, who was stirred as a youth toward awareness in the *Akedah,* seems in his old age to be unconscious of himself, to have sunk back into the state of the natural man. He would, by blessing Esau, follow the old way, assert the primacy of old principles that, in their inertia, discriminate against the individual in favor of the merely "natural." Isaac hears that the voice is Jacob's, but he is misled by his other senses, by feeling the hairy hand and by smelling the raiment. "See," he said, "the smell of my son is as the smell of a field the Lord hath blessed." Within the instant, and from the point of view of the transcendent theme and of the psyche's purpose, his blindness becomes a virtue: in wishing to follow the old way, he *does* follow it, relies on his animal senses and is tricked by them, and simultaneously tricks himself into serving the greater cause. His blessing meant for Esau is precisely what Jacob needs.

> . . . God give thee of the dew of heaven, and the fatness of the earth, and plenty of corn and wine:
>
> Let people serve thee, and nations bow down to thee: be lord over thy brethren, and let thy mother's sons bow down to thee: cursed be every one that curseth thee, and blessed be he that blesseth thee.
>
> Genesis 27:28–29

Jacob, the gentle unworldly man who lived in his tent and studied sacred lore, is given the promise of a life in every way opposite: remote from the outer order, he is promised deep roots in the earth; remote from men and practical circumstance, he is promised lordship over his brothers and leadership among nations. His humanity is to be made complete, and that is where his virtue will lie. Like all blessings, this one is part promise, part prophecy, a statement of the possible, something to be fulfilled. Jacob will spend a great many years under the burden of it.

When Jacob left his father's presence, a legend says

... he, by reason of the blessing he had received, came out crowned like a bridegroom; and the dew which is to revive the dead descended upon him from heaven, his bones became stronger, and he himself was turned into a mighty man.[77]

The legend completes the ritual: the glory of the man as he will be in the distant future is imagined to fall upon him in the present, as the blessing falls.

Esau came in from the hunt, bringing venison to Isaac.

> And Isaac his father said unto him, Who art thou? And he said, I am thy son, thy firstborn Esau.
>
> And Isaac trembled very exceedingly, and said, Who? where is he that hath taken venison, and brought it me, and I have eaten of all before thou camest, and have blessed him? yea, and he shall be blessed.
>
> Genesis 27:32–33

The curse Rebecca expected and chose to have fall upon herself is not uttered; Jacob's deceit and treachery go unpunished, except in the sense that the blessing was his punishment, since— like the Lord God's malediction against Adam—it cast him out into a life in all ways different from the life he had been leading. Esau cried out, hearing his father's question, with a "great and exceeding bitter cry," and begged for whatever blessing might be left.

> ... Bless me, even me also, O my father.
>
> And he said, Thy brother came with subtility, and hath taken away thy blessing.
>
> And he said, Is not he rightly named Jacob? for he hath supplanted me these two times: he took away my birthright; and, behold, now he hath taken away my blessing. And he said, Hast thou not reserved a blessing for me?
>
> And Isaac answered and said unto Esau, Behold, I have made him thy lord and all his brethren have I given to him for servants; and with corn and wine have I sustained him: and what shall I do now unto thee, my son?

And Esau said unto his father, Hast thou but one blessing, my father? bless me, even me also, O my father. And Esau lifted up his voice, and wept.

And Isaac his father answered and said unto him, Behold, thy dwelling shall be *away from* the fatness of the earth, and *away from* the dew of heaven from above;*

And by thy sword shalt thou live, and shalt serve thy brother; and it shall come to pass when thou shalt have the dominion, that thou shalt break his yoke from off thy neck.

Genesis 27:34–40

The true blessing seems always to have the same intent: like Adam, like Cain, like Jacob, Esau is cast out from all he knew and was lord over, cast out of a present and limited identity so that he might experience other facets of himself and of reality, and eventually be reconciled with his "brother." At this fine point, it is impossible to know what is blessing and what is curse; nothing but life, the course events take, the choices that are made and the actions that follow can ever clear up the matter. But in the long run each brother has the same destiny: each must experience his real relation with the other and each is promised by the blessing itself that in the fulfillment of his destiny he will find freedom. The future ultimately holds no question of dominion; neither will prevail. On the deepest level of meaning, what is destined is that the seemingly inimical principles of the inner order that Jacob and Esau symbolize will be found to be vitally related and reconciled in the name of freedom and wholeness. It will all take place in the midst of daily circumstance where, for the eye that really sees, the truth of it is again and again being proved.

And Esau hated Jacob because of the blessing wherewith his father blessed him: and Esau said in his heart, The days of mourning for my father are at hand; then will I slay my brother Jacob.

Genesis 27:41

* The italicized words do not appear in the King James Version, quoted here; but see Revised Standard and Goodspeed.

147

Though he might be thought to have the right to, Esau does not say in his heart, "then will I slay my father Isaac," and this omission is especially significant for the theoretician in the field of psychology. The poets of Genesis seem to have experienced the parental archetypes and the individual's relation with them in a way drastically different from that of the pagan poets, yet it is the latter whose insights have been considered so revelatory of what is innate in the human psyche.

Esau's words were said "in his heart," but Rebecca was told of them and she went to Isaac and persuaded him, by flimsy reasons, to send Jacob away to her brother Laban in Haran. When Jacob was ready to leave he was blessed again by his father.

> And God Almighty bless thee, and make thee fruitful, and multiply thee, that thou mayest be a multitude of people;
> And give thee the blessing of Abraham, to thee, and to thy seed with thee; *that thou mayest inherit the land wherein thou art a stranger, which God gave unto Abraham.* [My italics]
>
> Genesis 28:3–4

Jacob has not been particularly impressive up to now; certainly he has been lacking in the accepted virtues. He has been cradled in his tent, cared for and protected; he has been a conniver and—with Rebecca's help and only out of her vision—a trickster and deceiver. He does not seem to have suffered and in fact, even as he was acting according to the divine purpose, he seems to have experienced nothing. Evidently experience was not possible as long as he languished secure in the parental circle. As soon as he breaks away from it, goes out but also inward into the land "wherein thou art a stranger," Abraham's land, he comes quickly into his own distinct life and to a glimpse of that mystery according to which his destiny is to be fulfilled.

> And he lighted upon a certain place, and tarried there all night, because the sun was set; and he took of the stones of that place, and put them for his pillows, and lay down in that place to sleep.

And he dreamed, and behold a ladder set up on the earth, and the top of it reached to heaven: and behold the angels of God ascending and descending on it.

And, behold, the Lord stood above it, and said, I am the Lord God of Abraham thy father, and the God of Isaac: the land whereon thou liest, to thee will I give it, and to thy seed;

And thy seed shall be as the dust of the earth, and thou shalt spread abroad to the west, and to the east, and to the north, and to the south: and in thee and in thy seed shall all the families of the earth be blessed.

And, behold, I am with thee, and will keep thee in all places whither thou goest, and will bring thee again into this land; for I will not leave thee, until I have done that which I have spoken to thee of.

Genesis 28:11–15

In this great passage, the poetic spirit has struck as far inward as it is perhaps possible to strike: the mystery of the ladder rising up out of the sacred precinct will always be the abiding mystery that makes all things clear.

Jacob was shown, by means of the image of the ladder, which, set upon earth, reached with its top to heaven, how the worlds are connected with each other, how all things are interrelated, the things of heaven with the things of earth, the things of earth with those of heaven.[78]

Jacob woke, lifting his head from the first stone pillow he had ever been forced to sleep upon (it is as though the stones themselves invoked the dream), and said:

. . . Surely the Lord is in this place; and I knew it not.

And he was afraid, and said, How dreadful is this place! This is none other but the house of God, and this is the gate of heaven.

And Jacob rose up early in the morning, and took the stone that he had put for his pillows, and set it up for a pillar, and poured oil upon the top of it.

And he called the name of that place Beth-el: but the name of that city was called Luz at the first.

Genesis 28:16–19

The legends say that

God sank this anointed stone unto the abyss, . . . to serve as the centre of the earth, . . . the same stone, the Eben Shetiyah, that forms the centre of the sanctuary, whereon the Ineffable Name is graven, the knowledge of which makes a man master over nature, and over life and death.[79]

They also say this stone had once been the twelve stones of the altar upon which Isaac had been bound for the sacrifice; by a miracle the twelve stones became one and soft and downy like a pillow for Jacob's sake.[80]

The early commentators ask why the city Beth-el (i.e., House of God) was first called Luz and answer: "The town Luz is the heavenly Jerusalem in which dwells the majesty of God."[81]

Meister Eckhart wrote

He who knows and realizes how close to him (that is, in the soul) the Kingdom of God is, can say with Jacob, when he waked out of his sleep, "Surely the Lord is in this place and I knew it not."[82]

Jacob's words are full of youthful awe, but he seems as is usual with most of us to have had no inkling of what they really meant. The Voice had spoken, but it was a long time before he heard and much longer still before he saw. His story is very human. There is again and again in his life a marked hiatus between the vision that springs up within him and the working out of it in meaningful action.

When Jacob came to Haran, he came upon a well in a field and three flocks of sheep lying by it. It was the watering place for all the flocks of the countryside, but the combined strength of all the shepherds was necessary to roll back the great stone that blocked the well's mouth. As Jacob stood there, Rachel appeared with her father's sheep, and at the sight of her he went to the well and rolled back the stone and released the waters.[83] According to the legends, "the water rose from the depths of the well to the very top, there was no need to draw it up, and there it remained all the twenty years that Jacob abode in Haran."[84]

With this charming event, love rises from the depths of the psyche, and for the first time in the Book of Genesis the poetic spirit fully explores it as a dominant factor in human life.

> And Laban said unto Jacob, Because thou art my brother, shouldst thou therefore serve me for nought? tell me, what shall thy wages be?
>
> And Laban had two daughters: the name of the elder was Leah, and the name of the younger was Rachel.
>
> Leah was tender eyed; but Rachel was beautiful and well favoured.
>
> And Jacob loved Rachel; and said, I will serve thee seven years for Rachel thy youngest daughter.
>
> And Laban said, it is better that I give her to thee, than that I should give her to another man: abide with me.
>
> And Jacob served seven years for Rachel; and they seemed unto him but a few days, for the love he had to her.
>
> And Jacob said unto Laban, Give me my wife, for my days are fulfilled, that I may go in unto her.
>
> And Laban gathered together all the men of the place, and made a feast.
>
> And it came to pass in the evening, that he took Leah his daughter, and brought her to him; and he went in unto her.
>
> And Laban gave unto his daughter Leah Zilpah his maid for an handmaid.
>
> And it came to pass, that in the morning, behold, it was Leah: and he said to Laban, What is this thou hast done unto me? did not I serve with thee for Rachel? wherefore then hast thou beguiled me?
>
> And Laban said, It must not be so done in our country, to give the younger before the firstborn.

151

Fulfil her week, and we will give thee this also for
the service which thou shalt serve with me yet seven
other years.

And Jacob did so, and fulfilled her week: and he
gave him Rachel his daughter to wife also.

Genesis 29:15–28

The immediate gist of this would seem to be that you never
get by with anything: deceive and trick, and sooner or later others
will deceive and trick you. The rights of the first born are made
to prevail with the man who had seized them for himself. But here
again the spirit is playing with the figure, and to a much more
serious purpose than the moral lesson, valid though it may be
(and perhaps a good bit more than moral: our greatest tensions
often arise from the fact that our psychic dispositions trap us not
only in our privacy but in the world of action). Still, the motif is
what is important here and it started at the well, when the water
and love came springing up. What happened to Jacob at the well
is at bottom very like what happened when he dreamed about
the ladder: both were moments full of truth and of vision made
manifest. First on the level of the transcendental, then on the level
of the immediately human, he saw the image of his heart's desire;
the Word was uttered, within the inner order the individuality was
informed; but then, on waking, the long period of preparation
begins. The poets seem to say here that man may be, and is, given
the vision early, but nothing but long labor will restore it to him;
by nothing but long labor can he refine himself to the point at
which he is able to realize the vision's truth. More than twenty
years must pass before Jacob fully experiences the meaning of
his dream; though he worked for seven years in the very presence
of his love, it was not enough, for, as things turn out, he did not
really know her in his heart. On his wedding night, in the dark, he
proves to be very much his father's son and Esau's brother, a
"natural" man: though he heard Leah's voice, as Isaac had heard
his, he lets himself be tricked by his cruder senses. Leah the tender-
eyed is the embodiment of them.

The legends say that

Jacob therefore did not discover the deception

practised upon him until the morning. During the night Leah responded whenever he called Rachel, for which he reproached her bitterly when daylight came. "O thou deceiver, daughter of a deceiver, why didst thou answer me when I called Rachel's name?" "Is there a teacher without a pupil?" Leah asked in return. "I but profited by thy instruction. When thy father called Esau, didst thou not say, Here am I?"[85]

Jacob is not allowed to get by with anything, least of all the romantic aberration. The romantic lover, falling in love at first sight, like Jacob, may feel the world stop dead inside and out, and in the enchanting stillness that comes when the pairs of eyes have finally met, he may say all kinds of things he really means; but he always ends up with the same sad plea: "Don't change, never change, stay as you are, never let this moment end." It is not only that he naturally wants the image of his heart's desire to stay vivid and unaltered before him; he means something else as well. He always thinks the eyes that took him in took him whole, just as he was, and found him in no way lacking. So all of that stirring in the stillness, all of that awakening that seemed to him very like spring had its other side: the old primal inertia was at work, encouraging him to think he had sprung full-blown, whole, complete and perfected into the light of another's eyes; the image himself of another's heart's desire, and necessarily to be spared the demands of change. It is not love but inertia that is deceitful. In the first moment of love, the heart moves toward "the truly other," but that timeless moment ends, and the period afterwards is always long and laborious.

Jacob had to fulfill Leah's week, spend those days and nights with the opposite of the image of his desire; had to refine himself, as it were, out of the crudity of his senses before he could know as a man what had moved him at the well. Then he had seven years more work to do if he was to keep her. During this time he loved Rachel and detested Leah, but it was Leah who was fruitful; Rachel was barren.

> And when Rachel saw that she bare Jacob no children, Rachel envied her sister; and said unto Jacob, Give me children, or else I die.

And Jacob's anger was kindled against Rachel: and he said, Am I in God's stead, who hath withheld from thee the fruit of the womb?

Genesis 30:1–2

Is it his hatred which thwarts creativity, prevents the true and fruitful union with "the truly other"?

Jacob is angry, he cheats, he connives; he is cheated, tricked and connived against; Rachel sells him once to Leah in exchange for some mandrakes; Laban toys with his wages, makes bargains and tries to break them. It is the old daily human round and it is not broken until Rachel gives him a son whom she called Joseph. "And the Lord said unto Jacob, Return unto the land of thy fathers, and to thy kindred; and I will be with thee." (Genesis 31:3)

He stole away from Haran with his cattle, maidservants, menservants, camels, asses, and his wives and daughters and eleven of the twelve sons who would found the twelve tribes of Israel. Laban and his sons pursued him, ready for battle, but they made a covenant between them and parted in peace.

And Jacob went on his way, and the angels of God met him.

And when Jacob saw them, he said, This is God's host: and he called the name of that place Mahanaim.

And Jacob sent messengers before him to Esau his brother unto the land of Seir, the country of Edom.

And he commanded them, saying, Thus shall ye speak unto my lord Esau; Thy servant Jacob sayeth thus, I have sojourned with Laban, and stayed there until now:

And I have oxen, and asses, flocks, and menservants, and womenservants: and I have sent to tell my lord, that I may find grace in thy sight.

And the messengers returned to Jacob, saying, We came to thy brother Esau, and also he cometh to meet thee, and four hundred men with him.

Then Jacob was greatly afraid and distressed. . . .

Genesis 32:1–7

The angels who came to meet him may perhaps have been the same angels he saw in his dream, ascending and descending the ladder that stretched from earth to heaven, for he is about to experience the full meaning of that dream. He is about to confront his twin and shadow, that necessary task he has delayed for so long. The angels make their appearance, it seems, to let him know that he is re-entering the sacred precinct where he will have to face and do battle with himself.

The message he sent to Esau was hardly likely to bring him grace in his brother's sight, but he seems to have hoped that it would. When it fails, he, in his mortal fear, separates all his goods and flocks and followers into two companies, so that if one is destroyed one will be left; then he calls on the God of his fathers:

> I am not worthy of the least of all the mercies, and of all the truth, which thou has shewed unto thy servant; for with my staff I passed over this Jordan; and now I am become two bands.
>
> Genesis 32:10

As his fear overcomes him, he sends Esau a rich present—drove after drove of various cattle so spaced in their presentation as to wear down his brother's wrath and replace it with love of the donor, as though he himself, coming last, were the last and best part of the gift. He sends the droves over the brook Jabbok; then, in the night, he sends over the remaining flocks and his wives. With one quick gesture of command, one act of choice, he is separated from, and in a sense stripped of, all the fruits of his labors in Haran. Not even Rachel and the infant Joseph are left. On the bank of the brook Jabbok, in the dead of night, he is as alone as he was the night he left his father's tents and slept on the stone pillow.

> And Jacob was left alone; and there wrestled a man with him until the breaking of the day.
>
> And when he saw that he prevailed not against him, he touched the hollow of his thigh; and the hollow of Jacob's thigh was out of joint, as he wrestled with him.
>
> And he said, Let me go, for the day breaketh. And he said, I will not let thee go, except thou bless me.

And he said unto him, What is thy name? And he said, Jacob.

And he said, Thy name shall be called no more Jacob, but Israel: for as a prince hast thou power with God and with men, and hast prevailed.*

And Jacob asked him, and said, Tell me, I pray thee, thy name. And he said, Wherefore is it that thou dost ask after my name? And he blessed him there.

And Jacob called the name of the place Peniel: for I have seen God face to face, and my life is preserved.

And as he passed over Peniel the sun rose upon him, and he halted upon his thigh.

Genesis 32:24–31

Beyond Peniel, he met Esau, and Esau refused his gifts.

And Jacob said, Nay, I pray thee, if now I have found grace in thy sight, then receive my present at my hand: for therefore I have seen thy face, *as though I had seen the face of God,* and thou wast pleased with me. [My italics]

Genesis 33:10

In these few lines the levels of meaning are fused in a whole that encompasses and rounds out all the previous action. The warring brothers are reconciled. Both their lives seem to have been aimed directly toward the encounter on the banks of Jabbok, toward the battle in which neither vanquished the other, but he who was lord was blessed by his "servant."

> . . . until Jacob was at peace with the chieftain of Esau, Esau was not at peace with Jacob. For in all cases power below depends on the corresponding power above.[86]

The dark river lay there to be crossed. The "rivers" of the inner world most often symbolize a crucial obstacle, the crossing, the overcoming of which is necessary; this act must always be performed alone, on one's own, in utter self-reliance. Jacob met his

---

* ". . . he did not say 'thou hast prevailed *over* God,' but '*with* God,' i. e., to unite closely with God." *The Zohar,* translated by A. Sperling (London, The Soncino Press, 1932), Vol. II., Fol. 144b.

enemy on the riverbank, fought the night through against some-thing that could not or would not name itself, but could bless him ("for I have seen God face to face"), and in the sunlight beyond Peniel his adversary turns out to have been his brother, the twin he had tricked, cheated, fled from and, twenty years later, still quaked at the thought of meeting. But the face of Esau, the face of the shadow, the face of God are suddenly all the same in the sun that rises when the fight is over and the river crossed.

Jacob's is a hard-won virtue; he did not start with it, he had to discover and establish it out of his relations with both orders of experience, and this explains why (as the legend says) the "inner" world was then completed. His story represents a cycle that at the last is broken and lifts and spirals upward for the imagination. It begins in the realm of the family and of kindred partialities and de-ceits—where the psyche's inertia is most artfully concealed—and in the realm of the shadow; it swings out wide, curving through the constant interplay of the inner and outer orders of experience —a dream of a ladder and a vision of love at a well are as deeply significant as all the labor and the gain; and it swings back to the shadow at its darkest, back into the land of the "kindred" at its most profound; but with the encounter it is lifted into the light of peace and reconciliation.

In terms of the inner world, the story of this "virtuous" man seems to record perfectly those significant steps by which the indi-vidual experiences his relations with both orders of experience and comes to his unique situation—the human situation—at which, commingling, they lose all separateness and opposition. Taken as a whole symbolic action, it reveals the human psyche in its growth toward wholeness.

Jacob returned to Beth-El, the sacred precinct of his dream —after having "put away the strange gods"—to be confirmed in his new name, Israel, and to hear God reaffirm the blessing. As always, the blessing, reaffirmed, is a promise of creativity.

The Book of Genesis ends with the story of the eleventh son, Joseph, Jacob's beloved.

"Joseph is a fruitful bough, even a fruitful bough by a well, . . ." (Genesis 49:22)

Jacob could not leave Haran or break his servitude until after the birth of this "fruitful bough"; when, in Joseph, he had sired the future, God spoke to him and told him to go.

In Joseph's story the great themes are explored again, with even closer attention to the circumstances of daily life in which they must inevitably be worked out. The blessing is Joseph's from the beginning, and it is summed up in Jacob's gift to him of the coat of many colors, a symbol not only of his father's love but of the potential richness of the psyche; but that symbol, that potential, does not begin to aproach reality until it is drenched in blood. Like Abraham, like Jonah, like Christ, Joseph must spend a time in the heart of the earth, and Jacob would have liked to follow him there.

> And all his sons and all his daughters rose up to comfort him; but he refused to be comforted; and he said, For I will go down into the grave unto my son mourning. Thus his father wept for him.
>
> Genesis 37:35

But Joseph was lifted out of the heart of the earth into his destiny, and in the working out of that destiny he is very much Man himself, who must attend to his own becoming and bring himself to that creativity that even outlasts him and makes the fields and rivers fertile.

When Joseph has been sold into Egypt to Potiphar, the poets interrupt his story in order to tell that of his brother Judah who saved his life, saying "for he is our brother and our flesh." It is a story of the flesh and of sin—as though, approaching Joseph's glory, the poets would not have us forget the problems that abide in the human condition.

Judah had two sons and for the first, named Er, he chose a wife named Tamar. But Er "was wicked in the sight of the Lord; and the Lord slew him." Then Judah said to his second son, Onan, "Go in unto thy brother's wife," but Onan, not wishing to give seed to his brother, spilled his seed upon the ground. "And the thing which he did displeased the Lord: wherefore he slew him also." Then Judah kept Tamar a widow in his house until the time came when she knew he would never find another husband for her; she then took off her widow's clothes and covered her face like a harlot and sat in an open place until Judah approached her. Before she

would go with him, she demanded a pledge: his signet, his brace-
lets and his staff. She conceived by him, and when her time approached she was accused of harlotry; but when she was brought
forth she showed Judah's pledge and he acknowledged the objects
as his own. "And he knew her again no more."

> And it came to pass in the time of her travail, that,
> behold, twins were in her womb.
>
> And it came to pass, when she travailed, that the
> one put out his hand: and the midwife took and bound
> upon his hand a scarlet thread, saying, This came out
> first.
>
> And it came to pass, as he drew back his hand,
> that, behold, his brother came out: and she said, How
> hast thou broken forth? this breach be upon thee: there-
> fore his name was called Pharez.
>
> And afterward came out his brother, that had the
> scarlet thread upon his hand: and his name was called
> Zarah.
>
> Genesis 38:27–30

Earlier than this, after Jacob's return to Beth-El and Rachel's
death, there had been an incident with Reuben, the other of his
sons who had argued in favor of sparing Joseph's life:

> And it came to pass, when Israel dwelt in that land,
> that Reuben went and lay with Bilhah his father's con-
> cubine: and Israel heard it. . . .
>
> Genesis 35:22

The daily round, the seemingly inescapable human predicament, is all here: Judah, the murderous, incestuous father; the
wicked and the alien brothers; Tamar, the woman who must be
mother as well; the eternal warring twins; and Reuben, the incestuous son.

Origen, the great early Christian commentator, already
quoted at length with reference to Lot's daughters, wrote about
Reuben:

> No one is ignorant of the story of the incest, how
> Reuben was driven by the fire of lust to his father's con-
> cubine and stained his father's bed. . . .

In the first place, all men live carnally in this world, and are moved according to the flesh. The fleshly impulse is first in the concupiscence of lust which, when it besieges adolescence, makes the youth hard and rash and lustful at the same time . . . ascending even his father's bed and polluting the paternal couch. . . .

This is not all Origen has to say. I interrupt in order to make the point that he was writing some sixteen hundred years before Freud as he brought his remarks to a close.

". . . That is, acting contrary to the precepts and warnings of the natural law which is even now (i.e., in adulthood) . . ."

And he completes it:

"the paternal couch within us." *

The circle goes on turning back upon itself even as the individual—Abraham, Jacob, Joseph—discovers within himself the means to break and lift it. In reference to Reuben's sin, his guilt and healing, Jewish commentary says:

Then defiledst thou it! He went up to my couch. He perverted my couch, yet was healed.

His father said to him: "My son, thou canst have no healing until he comes of whom it is written, *And Moses went up unto God.*" (Exodus 19:3) And when Moses came and went up and stood on Mount Ebal, and appointed the tribe of Reuben first over the curses, and the tribe of Reuben opened their mouths and proclaimed, *Cursed be he that lieth with his father's wife* (Deuteronomy 27:20); then all Israel knew that Reuben was guiltless and was healed, and that the Holy One, blessed be He, had pardoned him.[87]

---

* "Incestus historia neminem latet, quomodo Ruben in concubinam patris efferbuerit flamma libidinis, et paternum maculaverit torum. . . .

Primo ergo omnis homo in hoc mundo carnaliter vivit et secundum carnem movetur. Et primus est carnalis motus in concupiscentia libidinus qui cum primae juventutis tempus obsederit durum et temerarium simul et lascivum juvenum reddit ascendentem etiam super cubile patris et polluentem torum paternum, id est, etiam praecepta et monita naturalis legis, quae in nobis est et nunc paternus torus dicitur, praevaricantem." Origen, *Homilia,* XVII, pp. 254–5.

As the Book of Genesis ends, with Joseph's death, all of Abraham's sons, the founders of the twelve tribes, are at home in Egypt. They have been there a long time under Joseph's protection. He had told them not to be afraid when, after Jacob's death, they had come expecting revenge from him:

> ... for am I in the place of God?
>
> But as for you, ye thought evil against me; but God meant it unto good, to bring to pass, as it is this day, to save much people alive.
>
> Now therefore fear ye not: I will nourish you, and your little ones. . . .
>
> So Joseph died, being an hundred and ten years old: and they embalmed him, and he was put in a coffin in Egypt.
>
> Genesis 50:19–21; 26

In the remaining four books of the Pentateuch, the poets render their themes, not primarily in the story of a great individual, but in the story of the people themselves. The people, all of the Israelites, undergo what has been suffered by the individual alone. "In order to do what he has done today: save the lives of many people," the Israelites are cast down, brought to their own experience of brutality and evil and of the pit. In spite of all the rules and regulations, laws and ritual practices concerning the people as a whole with which these four books are concerned, the underlying themes and the dominant passion remain the same. In Deuteronomy, the last book, it is the whole people who have been brought to "this Jordan" Jacob had to cross; and on the other side, in the terms of the Covenant, lies the "land flowing with milk and honey."

The eve of the crossing is given over to Moses; it is his time to recapitulate all that has happened to the people since they left Egypt, and to hand down to them the Law he received from God's hand on Mount Sinai. The people's turn has come to write the law *for themselves:* crossing over into the land of awareness necessarily means crossing into the land of responsibility.

> And thou shalt write upon them all the words of this law, when thou art passed over, that thou mayest go

161

in unto the land which the Lord thy God giveth thee, a land that floweth with milk and honey; as the Lord God of thy fathers hath promised thee.

Deuteronomy 27:3

After the crossing, they will pass between two mountains:

These shall stand upon mount Gerizim to bless the people, when ye are come over Jordan: Simon and Levi, and Judah, and Issachar, and Joseph, and Benjamin:

And these shall stand upon mount Ebal to curse: Reuben, Gad and Asher, and Zebulun, Dan and Naphtali."

Deuteronomy 27:12–13

That this should happen is part of the Covenant:

... that is how those did it, who entered into a covenant: they erected a partition wall to the right and left and passed through the middle; as it is said in Jeremiah 34: 18, "they cut the calf in twain and passed between the parts thereof." [88]

The imaginative leap the commentator, Rashi, takes here, from the parts of the calf to the partition walls to the two mountains across Jordan, daring as it is, is sustained by man, the common denominator of the three rites, who passes through the middle. In the Bible, Man is always in the middle, in between the world's oppositions, the blessing and the curse, for he has the gift of choice and the responsibility for it, the gift and power of self-knowledge and all it entails in the world of action.

"Cursed be he that maketh the blind to wander out of the way." (Deuteronomy 27:18)

This is a salient curse and one of the most important messages to be found in the Old Testament, for there is implicit in it the certainty, the unshakable conviction, that for the individual knowledge and choice and responsibility are so intimately related as to be inextricable one from the other. This conviction has served to guide and to motivate much of modern depth psychology as a science, although we have in general been unconscious of the fact, and even of the source of the message, and have sought its meaning elsewhere, in mythological and legendary sources of paler insight.

The other curses the Israelites are to hear as they pass mount Ebal are all directed at the daily round and the persistent facts of the human condition:

> Cursed be he that lieth with his father's wife; because he uncovereth his father's skirt. And all the people shall say, Amen.
>
> Cursed be he that lieth with any manner of beast. . . .
>
> Cursed be he that lieth with his sister, the daughter of his father, or the daughter of his mother. . . .
>
> Cursed be he that lieth with his mother in law. And all the people shall say, Amen.
>
> Deuteronomy 27:20–23

The people are told how to conduct themselves in all ways, yet the balance, the sense of harmony between the known and the unknown, and the sense of human strength and frailty, is perfectly sustained:

> "Yet the Lord hath not given you an heart to perceive, and eyes to see, and ears to hear, unto this day.
>
> The secret things belong unto the Lord our God: but those things which are revealed belong unto us and to our children forever, that we may do all the words of this law.
>
> Deuteronomy 29:4, 29

In his final warning to his people, Moses commands them to "turn unto the Lord thy God *with all thine heart and with all thy soul,*" and then he sums up all that has been discovered about the ultimate sources of value and of responsibility and of creativity. He sets before them "life and death, blessing and cursing: therefore choose life, that both thou and thy seed may live."

> For this commandment which I command thee this day, *it is not hidden from thee* [my italics], neither is it far off.
>
> It is not in heaven, that thou shouldest say, Who

Figure 14. Moses striking the rock;
the Israelites' idolatry of the brazen serpent

shall go up for us to heaven, and bring it unto us, that we may hear it, and do it?

Neither is it beyond the sea, that thou shouldest say, Who shall go over the sea for us, and bring it unto us, that we may hear it, and do it?

But the word is very nigh unto thee, in thy mouth, and in thy heart, that thou mayest do it. [My italics]

See, I have set before thee this day life and good, and death and evil.

Deuteronomy 30:11–15*

Before his death, Moses went up mount Nebo and the Lord God showed him the promised land:

. . . This is the land which I sware to Abraham, unto Isaac, and unto Jacob, saying, I will give it unto thy seed: I have caused thee to see it with thine eyes, thou shalt not go over thither.

So Moses the servant of the Lord died there in the land of Moab according to the word of the Lord.

Deuteronomy 34:4–5

It is awesome, this reversal of the outcome of the great theme. Tragedy, in the Greek sense, falls to Moses, the heir to all the riches of the individual, from Adam to Abraham, Jacob to Joseph. In spite of the fact that it was through his vision and through his intimacy with his God that the Israelites were brought to Jordan and the shore of the land of promise, it is he, Moses, no one else, who is denied that land. Depth of vision, depth of awareness, depth of responsibility: let all three be as profound as they may be, but, the poets seem to say here, the more profound each becomes, the more significant and critical each moment and each action taken in it becomes; the closer one comes to refinement of vision, the closer to full awareness, the more certain does it become that a single failure, a single instance of the neglect of faith will be enough to assure that one will be denied the ultimate experience of one's own vision. For Moses the fatal instant came when, relying on *reason alone* and on the image of himself as leader of the people, he took his rod and struck the rock. The failure, the lapse,

* See II Corinthians 3:3 and Romans 2:14–15.

the fear of the risk to entrust oneself to the *Word also* proves that the eternal round has not been broken. The flaw in Moses and in his relationship with his people persisted in the inner world and was manifested in the people's idolatry of the Nehustan, the brazen serpent, which symbolized for them not the power of the Word but the power of Moses as leader, until it was destroyed.

Nevertheless, for the poets of the Bible tragedy may always be averted. It is always a question of choice and responsibility and of action on the basis of what man is, in all his gifts and attributes, and what he may be. For these poets, existence was always meaningful, man was always human, and it was in his very humanity, in his relation with himself, with his fellow men, with the universe and with God that his freedom and his creativity and his very destiny were to be found.

Tomorrow shall be, shall be my dancing day,
I would my true love did so chance to see the legend of
    my play,
To call, to call my true love to my dance.

Sing, oh, my love, my love, my love, my love,
This have I done for my true love.

Then was I born of a Virgin pure, of her I took my
    fleshly substance;
Thus was I knit to man's nature,
To call, to call my true love to my dance.

Sing, oh, my love, oh, my love, my love, my love,
This have I done for my true love.

In a manger laid and wrapped I was, so very poor,
this was my chance,
Betwixt an ox and a silly poor ass,
to call, to call my true love to my dance.

Then afterwards baptiz'd I was,
The Holy Ghost on me, on me did glance,
My Father's voice, my Father's voice heard from above,
To call, to call my true love to my dance.

Into the desert I was led, where I fasted without
    substance;
The Devil bade me make bread, from stones,
To have me break, to have me break my true love's
    dance.
. . . .
Then down to Hell I took my way,
For my true love's, for my true love's deliverance,
And rose, and rose again on the third day,
Up to my true love, up to my true love and the dance.

Then up to Heav'n I did ascend, Where now I dwell in
    pure substance,
On the right hand of God, that man may come, may
    come unto the gen'ral dance.
(From a mediaeval British lyric, Anonymous 15th–16th century

PART THREE

The Case of Joan

Introduction
BY SIR HERBERT READ

THE AUTHOR of this book, the "observer-participant" in the case of Joan, has given such a detailed and sympathetic commentary on the course of the analysis that there is little left to say, even from my special point of view, which is that of a philosopher of art. Any study of the history of art, and especially a consideration of the function of art in our own distracted age, leaves me with a conviction of the existence of an intimate relation between art and social integration. Art in its widest sense has become almost the sole outlet for those constructive energies that enable the psyche to condition itself to an objective harmony. By this I mean that the distracted spirit of man, by practising (and to a lesser extent by appreciating) an art, may seek and find an integration of his mind and his sensibility, of extraversive and introversive tendencies; and that society as a whole may be united in the common pursuit of beauty. These remain vague ideals, but the therapeutic value of the practice of an art is not in doubt: the only question is why psychiatrists do not avail themselves more often of its aids.

The case of Joan is significant, first because it is a successful example of art therapy in a difficult case; and then because the by-products of the treatment are of great artistic interest. The kind of comparison one could make with great masterpieces is perhaps facile, but some of the drawings remind me forcibly, perhaps of a

169

painting by El Greco, perhaps of Picasso's *Demoiselles d'Avignon*. That is to say, they have the compulsive vitality that characterizes art in its most permanent features, combined with a tendency toward coherent form which gives the work of art its universality. In the case of the professional artist one must suppose some conscious calculation of such effects, but in the case of Joan both order and vitality seem to come from a formative principle in the unconscious.

Joan was exceptional in that she had had some artistic training before the treatment began; the psychotherapist could therefore rely on a certain skill or facility in the task of self-expression. Though there were inhibitions to overcome, they were not the inhibitions that afflict the normal patient who protests that "he cannot draw for toffee." It is possible that from the therapist's point of view aesthetic quality is of little importance. He is normally seeking for symbolic representations of hidden conflicts, and the plainer these are and the less "aestheticised" the better. This is where I would like to support Mr. Westman in his conviction that "the psyche is a complex of energies and inertias not only potentially harmonious, balanced and whole, but actually in its ontogenesis *determined upon* the achievement of harmony, balance and wholeness." There should be no difficulty in supposing that a tendency of this kind is built into the human organism; that in this respect the human organism does not differ from a sea shell, a flower or a crystal. In any case, the difference between a healthy psyche and a sick one is the difference between order and disorder, harmony and chaos, and the problem for the psychiatrist is to restore the mental functioning of the patient to a balance that is not merely ideal, but natural.

The quality of the drawings produced by Joan in the course of treatment is such that a hasty judgment might conclude that a measure of psychosis is good for the artist. Certainly one cannot exclude conflict from the formative influences in art—art does not proceed from inertia. But we must distinguish between skill and invention. Skill is physical; in an art like drawing, a muscular coordination of hand and eye. It may be innate or it may be a product of training, but its psychiatric significance is negligible, as I have already implied. But invention is a function of the mind, of the imagination; and the imagination is energized by conflict. The work of art is a resolution of such conflicts in the terms of universal values. On the dynamic level such values are known as harmony, rhythm, balance, proportion; but there is also an archetypal level on which the resolution is in terms of dream and myth, and the integration is deep and permanent to the degree that these two levels are brought together, so that dream and myth are heightened into orphic song or tragic drama. What Joan accomplished in the course of an analysis, besides being a graphic record of her gradual recovery, is also a progression towards an art rich in reconciling images for all mankind.

The Case of Joan

THE PATIENT is on the borderline of a psychotic break
which, should it occur, would probably be manic and
severe in nature. There is evidence of marked paranoia
and of being a split personality from early childhood.

Joan, the patient referred to in this summation by the testing
psychologist, was nineteen years old at the time, the second of
three daughters of middle-class parents. Her father is a store-
keeper, her mother a good housewife. Honest, well-meaning people, they were hopeful that Joan, like her sisters, would grow up
healthy and happy, have a good job as a stenographer and marry
quickly. She had, however, a talent for drawing, and when she
finished high school she was registered in a commercial art school;
but she did not go to her classes. She ran away and roamed the
countryside, came back to the city and lived like a derelict for
nearly two years. When she appeared at the psychiatric outpatient
department of a New York hospital, she was, as the psychologist's
report indicates, in very grave distress. She looked strong, she was
well and solidly built, but she was shabby and dirty, and she was
wholly withdrawn. She had unusual facial mannerisms, a one-
sided smile, for example, which scarcely moved her lips. Her eyes
were blank.

Joan was given a battery of tests. She rated 109 on the verbal
scale, 113 on performance; her arithmetic score was very low.*
No evidence emerged of hereditary factors in relation to mental illness. Speaking of her parents during an early interview, she said
she did not believe they loved her "beyond the sort of love one
gives to something one owns." Later, her mother admitted having
had difficulties nursing her from the beginning. Joan described her
father as cold but intelligent. When he was told his daughter had

* The specialist's attention is directed to the comparative psychological report reprinted as an appendix.

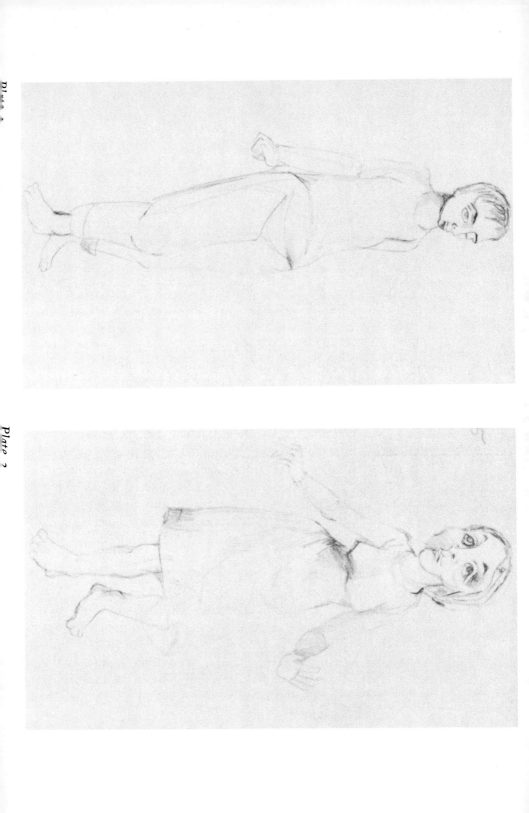

Plate 1

Plate 2

Plate 3

a remarkable artistic talent, he answered, "All what I got in her is a crazy artist, eh?"

Asked in the routine of tests to draw a picture, she replied that she was an art student and so whatever she drew would be "just art." Coming from someone in deep depression, this was a highly significant statement and the decision to attempt to treat her by psychotherapy hinged partly upon it. It meant she thought she had to justify her interest in art by always drawing pictures others would call "artistic," but it also meant that somehow she knew better; that her real need was to use her gifts in her own way, as she must, according to her own nature, never minding whether the picture was "art" or not.

She drew a man and a woman (Plates 1 and 2) and then she drew a woman in the rain. (Plate 3) In reference to the latter she said, "It's obvious as hell. She is obviously lost . . . you could tell that."

Her treatment began in November, 1955. During the first six months, Joan came to see me at the hospital once a week; thereafter I saw her twice weekly, once at the hospital and once at my office. Her pictures reproduced here in exact chronological order are selected from all the work she did from the beginning of her treatment until late in 1957. The date of composition is indicated in many cases, in order to show the time lapse between drawings. The pictures omitted from this selection were repetitious, simply statements and restatements of the same theme.

To provide a background in art for this theme and a kind of summation of it, there are included here reproductions of two paintings by Hieronymus Bosch and an illumination from the Kennicott Bible.

Plate 4

"The Cure of Folly" is the first painting of the two by Bosch. Here, as early as the fifteenth century, the artist questions the treatment of mental illness by "science." Against a landscape that I take to symbolize the inner world itself, the doctor tries to cure the sick man by extracting the "stone of madness"—it seems to be an early experiment in leucotomy! The nun watches, using the Bible for a hat; the Holy Book means nothing to her except as a covering for her head. Bosch seems to say that she, like the sick

Plate 4. Hieronymus Bosch, The Cure of Folly

man, has forgotten that there are substances more subtle than stone. The circular composition is framed by an inscription that leaves no doubt about the artist's meaning: the folly consists in human physics' attempting to reclaim the psyche that has forgotten its origins, its nature and its destiny.

"Master, cut out the stone my name is the everlasting dupe." (The phrase, literally translated, is "gilded dog.")

Plate 5

"The Seven Deadly Sins" is composed as a mandala, the Eastern artistic form already referred to as symbolic of the experience of wholeness. "The very form affected by the composition amplifies its moral intent," Jacques Combes writes in his study of Bosch. "Bosch would seem to raise the symbolism of his art to the height of universality by means of circular composition." [89] The great rose windows of mediaeval cathedrals symbolize pure holiness in "wholeness," but here Bosch creates a mandala that symbolizes the potential wholeness of the psyche in terms of the relations of its various human aspects. The Seven Deadly Sins are enlightened, as it were, by Christ at the center; in other words, their meaning and the meaning of all that is seemingly deadly within us is to be arrived at only in relation with the awareness for which Christ is the purest image.

Plate 6

The Kennicott Bible was illustrated by a Jewish artist roughly contemporary with Bosch. His mandala is like the Flemish artist's in that the holy is the center, but the Christian sees it as *God-Man* while the former sees it abstractly, not to be depicted, but surrounded by the beast. The experience, however, is very much the same: wholeness perforce includes both light and dark, sin and virtue, beast and spirit, and humanity lies in the very experience and realization of it. The Seven Deadly Sins and the beast are equivalent symbols for the artists' experience of aspects of reality of the inner world as well as the outer; both are images of those forces that threaten the intrinsic individuality until relations with them are established. But both pictures are resolutions of the conflict; as mandalas, they reveal the artist's glimpse of the essential harmony of the inner world, which comes when all its forces are integrated with its true center.

Plate 5. Hieronymus Bosch, The Seven Deadly Sins

Plate 6. *Mandala, from the Kennicott Bible*

The dramatic conflict implicit in all of Joan's early work is here: in the experiences of the primal forces themselves and in the struggle, by virtue of the very nature of the psyche itself, to establish harmony between them in the name of the single, isolated human individuality.

Plate 7: Dec. 6, 1955

The difference between this drawing and Joan's first three is immediately obvious. The first three could not have been drawn by a psychotic patient; neither, in fact, could this—but it shows that she is perilously close. It is as though she had held on to herself just long enough to draw the man, the woman, and the woman in the rain, in that disciplined, terse and economical way; then, having found in the psychotherapeutic situation a mite of hope, she had simply let go. The line is shattered. The atmosphere is stark and menacing; the imagination is depicted in chains. The drawing shows the direction her vital energies have taken and gives some indication of what she is going to suffer; it is a rendering of the first hesitant step into psychosis. The diagnosis of the testing psychologist is confirmed. There is not only great danger of a lapse into a severe catatonic state, but in a subtle sense that lapse has already taken place. The fact is that with this drawing she begins to render her experience of the forces of her psyche, those energies that have dominated her *as an individual* and have brought her to her plight. There is only a hint of this experience in the first three drawings, in the subtle distortions of the figures, in the attitude of the woman "obviously lost." Now Joan is in the very midst of the experience, but, by the drawing itself, she somehow holds onto that mystery we call the *human*. She is led to picture her own hope in the blades of grass at the foot of the chained winged figure and in the flower. These biological symbols are the only signs of life and they serve as a kind of point of view for the whole drawing, making it a rendering of an experience rather than simply the gifted scribbling of a girl who is mentally ill. They are symbolic of what remains of her shattered personality, that frail means by which up to now she has, however wretchedly, been related with existence. That she could draw them gave some hope for the establishment of personality in terms of her own individuality and for its growth.

Plate 8: Jan. 27, 1956

To think of schizophrenia in terms of its etymology ("split mind") is not very helpful:

The human psyche is a complex of energies and inertias variously conditioned and directed, released and dammed up, utilized and neglected, unsuspected, repressed. Precisely as our cellular energies are directed toward the orderly and harmonious realization and functioning of the physical organism, precisely as cosmic energies seem to work toward the harmony of the universe, so do the energies of the psyche in its ontogenesis work toward harmony and order and the goal of wholeness. Neither in the universe nor in the physical organism nor in the psyche is there a discoverable center: in all three the integration is ineffably mysterious. In Analytical Psychology, we posit as the center of the psyche the Self, the source of man's intrinsic individuality and its guide. But we can really only talk about the means toward integration of the energies and inertias of the psyche, and this means is what I have called personality.

It is not, in the long run, a question of whether the psyche is "split"; in terms of the above definition, the psyche would always be "split" to some degree, for the goal of wholeness itself necessarily means wholeness *in change, in the midst of the natural order, the old but continuously new and lively.* The question is rather to what extent the intrinsic individuality is able to assert itself in the midst of the forces of the inner world, to what extent it is fed and nurtured and sustained by them, rather than driven and ruled; to what extent, in other words, there is *personality.* In mental illness, personality is what breaks down. In schizophrenia the various aspects of the personality (the various relations with the forces of the outer and inner worlds) split away from each other in radical dissociation that may exhibit many shades and gradations and may be quite systematic or wholly unsystematic. This drawing of Joan's depicts critical dissociation of the unsystematic kind. She draws herself in depression and utter bewilderment, holding her head in her hands in a posture exactly descriptive of the catatonic state threatened in Plate 7. Everything around her is out of joint. Outside, separate from her vision of herself as consciously depressed, weird figures grow one from the other, and strange shapes

late 8

crowd into the scene with no hint of system or design. But on the head of one of the figures the blades of grass reappear.

Plates 9 and 10: Feb. 16 and 23, 1956

Often during the schizophrenic process, depending upon the degree of severity, it happens that energy is concentrated in a certain force or in certain forces of the psyche, and a kind of autonomy is established; a part comes to rule the rest, and the patient *lives* a single aspect of his humanity as if it were the whole. Symptomatic, for example, of pathological states of schizophrenia is the patient's tendency to identify with messianic figures, with prophets or with political or otherwise powerful public personalities, or even with animals. In Joan's case, the stone-throwing figure in Plate 9 reveals symbolically such a concentration of energy in a single aspect of the psyche that intends to rule the rest. The figure first appeared in her childhood; here, at a very early stage in her psychotherapy, it re-emerges to become a kind of companion that accompanies her in many disguises throughout her treatment. Destructive, obstructive, negative, resistant, the figure as drawn is a realization of the archetypal inertia. Powerful as it appears to be and literally is, it is by a curious paradox the product of the inertia inherent in the psyche. In a subtle way, that inertia is active here, presenting itself to the imagination in a symbol of power that is the very obverse of its true nature, yet perfectly expressive of the threat it constitutes to human individuality. There is another level of meaning also: our most energetic and powerful actions are often no more than the products of our primal inertia, and as such they are invariably destructive to personality.

Joan wrote on the back of Plate 9, "The Descent," and she was right. Her energies have turned downward or backward to the beginnings of the psyche (Plate 10), to that original state that is neither "dreaming innocence" nor paradise, but *chaos in simultaneity.* Everything is potential here, nothing is actual, nothing human except in that it is *all* human, a view of the primal ground, the *Urgrund,* as it were, before the Word was uttered. Joan draws herself at the bottom of the scene, near the center, in a posture very like that of the "woman in the rain," as though this present chaos is what also surrounds the earlier figure and explains why she is "obviously lost."

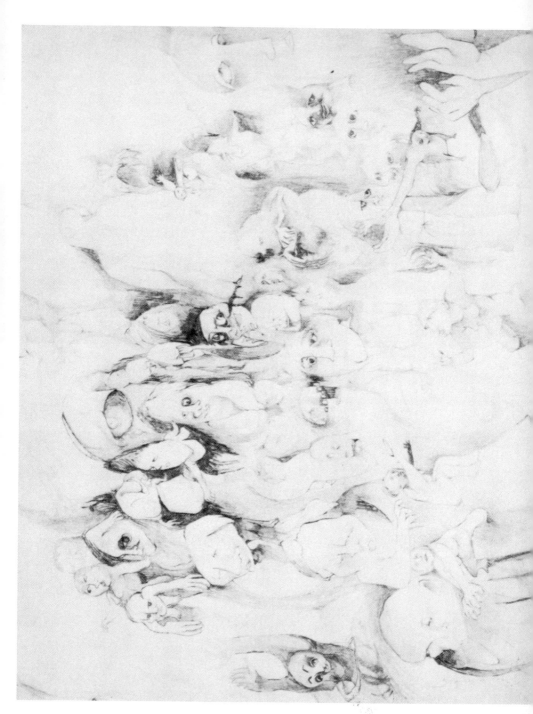

Plate 10

When she drew this view of the primal ground, Joan was not remembering; it is not the past that is recaptured here. As far as the psyche is concerned, time is the least of things. The primal ground is eternally present; it is the ultimate foundation of the instant, the locale within which we experience the timeless.

> When above the heaven had not (yet) been named,
> (And) below the earth had not (yet) been called by
>   name;
> (When) Apsû primeval, their begetter,
> Mummu, (and) Tiâmat, she who gave birth to them all,
> (Still) mingled their waters together,
> And no pasture land had been formed (and) not (even)
>   a reed marsh was to be seen;
> When none of the (other) gods had been brought into
>   being,
> (When) they had not (yet) been called by (their)
>   names,
> And their destinies had not (yet) been fixed,
> (At that time) were the gods created within them.
>   *Enuma Elish,* Tablet I, 1–9[90]

The *Enuma Elish* contains a great deal that is important for the understanding of Joan's case. It is apparently the earliest Babylonian creation myth, a kind of *Ur*-myth, and it is as directly concerned with the origins and growth of the psyche as is the Book of Genesis. Its dramatic motifs are prototypical of much that is familiar to us in other myths of other peoples.*

As Joan draws the primal ground, it is analagous to that described by the Babylonian poets. The waters are still mingled together; the primal forces are undifferentiated; there is no sexuality. The experience in the garden ("And they saw that they were naked") has not taken place. There has, in fact, been no "seeing," no action on the basis of the intrinsic individuality (that *presupposition of our humanity*) by virtue of which we enter the primal realm on our own terms in order to understand ourselves through ourselves. This is the true *original* human situation, before the

* The *Enuma Elish* is not considered here as the *source* of these motifs. It deals with universal human experience, which it renders in familiar symbolic patterns, archetypes of individual development.

The Springs of Creativity

Word has been uttered, the ear has heard, the eye has seen. It has nothing to do with conflicts between matriarchal and patriarchal culture patterns; such rationalizations may be useful to anthropologists and to some social psychologists, but they remain "analytical" constructs and have nothing to do with the deepest human experience.*

Inherent in the original human situation is the original conflict—the conflict between the force that strives toward wholeness, and thus toward creativity, and the inertia that strives to maintain chaos and thwart growth and creativity.

> Apsû opened his mouth
> And said to Tiâmat in a loud voice:
> ". . . By day I cannot rest, by night I cannot sleep!
> I will destroy (them) and put an end to their way,
> That silence be established, and then let us sleep!"
>   Tablet, I, 35–40

Apsu is crying out against his first born, the gods, who have been disturbing "the inner parts of Tiamat, Moving and running about in the divine abode (?)" (Tablet I, 23–24). The poet is really talking about his own experience of the primal conflict; the cry is the cry of his own inertia. It is very important that the father, Apsu, is made to utter it; again and again the poets have chosen the negative parent as a symbol of inertia, and they have symbolized the conflict between that inertia and their own creativity, not as a situation of "love" between son and mother, but as the act of patricide. What is true of the other great pagan mythological dramas is true of the *Enuma Elish:* love as a *motive* is nonexistent.

> When Tiamat heard Apsu's cry,
> She was wroth and cried out to her husband;
> She cried out and raged furiously, she alone.
> She pondered the evil in her heart (and said):
> "Why should we destroy that which we ourselves have
>   brought forth?

* The reader who is familiar with Dr. Erich Fromm's *The Forgotten Language* will quickly see that the following interpretation of the *Enuma Elish* is in diametric opposition to Dr. Fromm's.

188

Their way is indeed very painful, but let us take it good-
naturedly!"

Tablet, I, 42–46

But like Cronos, Apsu went on plotting the murder of his
children, only to be murdered instead by his son, Ea, as Laius was
murdered by Oedipus. Then, like Jocasta, Tiamat took her son,
Kingu, as her husband.

She gave him the tablet of destinies, she fastened (it)
upon his breast, (saying:)
"As for thee, thy command shall not be changed, (the
word of thy mouth) shall be dependable!"

Tablet I, 156–157

The tablet she gave her "unique spouse" gave him the power
to create reality by the spoken word. Then, to avenge Apsu, Tiamat got ready for war against their children. Her son Marduk
came forth as their champion. He had already proved to have by
virtue of his own individuality the power the tablet of destinies
was supposed to confer on Kingu.

"Thy destiny, O lord, shall be supreme among the gods.
Command to destroy and to create, (and) they shall be!
By the word of thy mouth, let the garment be destroyed;
Command again, and let the garment be whole!"
He commanded with his mouth, and the garment was
destroyed.
He commanded again, and the garment was restored.

Tablet IV, 21–27

Before the battle, Marduk spoke to his mother, Tiamat, in
a way very familiar to psychotherapists:

"Why dost thou act (so) friendly on the surface,
While thine heart is plotting to stir up strife?
The sons have rebelled (and) maltreat their father;
And thou, their bearer, hatest mercy."

Tablet IV, 77–80

Tiamat lost the battle, Marduk killed her, and then:

189

He took from him [Kingu] the tablet of destinies,
which was not his rightful possession. [My italics]

Tablet IV, 121

Marduk called the great gods to an assembly and asked:

"Who was it that created the strife,
And caused Tiâmat to revolt and prepare for battle?"
Let him who created the strife be delivered up; . . .
. . . the great gods answered him:
"Kingu it was who created the strife,
And caused Tiâmat to revolt and prepare for battle."
They bound him and held him before Ea;
Punishment they inflicted upon him by cutting
(the arteries of) his blood.
With his blood they created mankind; . . . [My italics]*

Tablet VI, 23–25, 29–33

The Babylonian poets probed to an astonishing depth into the human situation. They differ from the poets of Genesis in that they could not conceive of a time when there was *nothing but God;* they were therefore compelled to set down their experiences in terms of cosmic events. Nevertheless, from the psychologist's point of view, their work is not only one of humanity's earliest but one of its most valid efforts to reveal the way of the psyche in its onto-genesis. It seems to me that Apsu and Tiamat symbolize the primal state, the chaos of the potential. Kingu symbolizes that mode of action of the psyche by which it identifies itself with and depends wholly upon parental images. In him the Babylonian poets anticipate by some four thousand years Freud's hypothesis (i.e, identification with parental images as evidenced in the Oedipus complex), which is now taken as scientifically proven. Kingu is, however, more than this: he is an extension of the Apsu-inertia motif, and the poets rightly condemn him to death. But, most significant of all, they knew mankind was created from *his* blood—knew, in other words, that what he represents is an inherent part of our human nature.

Marduk would seem to be a symbol of emergent individuality; in him, as an ideal, the poets anticipate the growth of per-

* See Part II, pages 77–81; John 9:6; and Genesis 2:7.

sonality, that subtle means by which individuality becomes creative of its own accord. His destruction and re-creation of the garment by the power of the Word alone demonstrates his relation with the powers of Being, as well as his independence.* His battle with Tiamat is a dramatization of this independence and a testing of the powers he demonstrated in the incident of the garments. His victory was certain before the battle started, but it was necessary that the psychic "fact" be experienced as an event in the world of action. The signal difference between Marduk and Kingu is that the latter is guilty of *hubris,* that "overweening pride" that is truly an idolatry of the personal image; it leads him to accept from his mother that which is not hers to give nor his rightfully to take. Behind his *hubris* stands the more "original" sin of inertia by which he depends upon a parental image for an identity whose power is symbolized in the tablet of destinies.

Inertia often shows itself and its influence in modern life in such a complex symbol as this. It is original "sin" because it thwarts the psyche in its ontogenesis, hampers the development of personality and thus thwarts creativity and leads us to fail the creation of which we are a part.

Like Jacob, Marduk conquered himself and won the power of creativity, and proceeded to impose order upon the primal chaos. This divine act of creation would seem to be the poet's image of his own experience, of what he himself went through when order first came into the chaos of his beginnings; when, out of the inevitable conflict between the creative forces within him and the inertia which is their natural counterpart, he glimpsed in the order of the cosmos the possibility of order within himself, and the hope for wholeness.

The conflict between creativity and inertia in the inner world, this fundamental problem of our existence, is resolved, the reader will remember, in a markedly different way in the Book of Genesis. The key to the later, more radical and human resolution, is in the idea of the one God and of Man's most intimate relation with him. There is no patricide in the Jacob-Esau story, and there is no "identification" with the mother; there is rather the opposite. It is through the blind father's blessing and the mother's willingness to take a curse upon herself that the individuality of the son is urged

* See Numbers 20:12, and page 53 of this book.

forward into action, the personality given the opportunity to develop, the psyche freed to the realization of its purpose.

The meaning of the *Enuma Elish* is directly applicable to Joan's case. She wrote a message on the back of Plate 10:

> "Don't feel a thing, am in an ugly mood now. Something has got to change . . . and soon . . . very, very soon. I will die this way. I am too lonely."

There is nothing lonelier than the primal realm of Apsu and Tiamat, and few descents are more dangerous to undertake. But there is another side of the picture: hesitant, tentative, even dim, this drawing (Plate 10) is nevertheless a view, from a different angle, of the sacred precinct. This is not by any means an image of an experience suffered solely by the schizophrenic. In a very real sense, in his own way, every artist "descends" to varying depths, depending upon his inner strength, into the primal realm where he experiences the *self-realizing and self-manifesting agency* of his origins. In doing so, he risks himself, and this is a very difficult and painful and dangerous experience: he gives up his hard-won "objectivity" in favor of the forces at work within him; he lets go his firm grip on the "reality" and security of his identifications and his mask, for his goal is self-discovery and self-revelation in the deepest sense. Naturally, in the process he suffers grave anxieties about existence itself; as he approaches the creative act, the very sense he has of *being,* of an individuality somehow independent but related with the forces of both worlds, is threatened and seems to dwindle; and yet, in the midst of the creative act, in the instant of self-discovery, both *being* and *existence* are reaffirmed in a way he has not known before. All of this is reflected in what we call the temperament of the artist.*

In Joan's case this problem is a matter of extremity. Her anxiety was enormous, and it was in every way healthy that she felt it. There was great danger that, having descended into the primal realm, she would never come out of it. The moment she entered it, she encountered a destructive "spirit" (Plate 9), a stone thrower who threatened to become autonomous and prevent any possibility of cure. The stone thrower corresponds to Apsu and he meant literally to kill her as a person—to keep her, in other

* See Mr. Andrew Lytle's fine, moving essay, "The Working Novelist," *Daedalus,* April, 1959.

words, in his realm, inert at the center of violent energies. The next picture (Plate 10) is full of energy pouring out and spending itself in unnamed, mindless creation; the crowds of figures are simply events, things happening in the primal situation in which there is as yet no means by which the intrinsic individuality can relate itself with the powers that might sustain it. But the descent and the encounter with the stone thrower were necessary experiences for Joan, as they are, to a degree, necessary for all of us. The stone thrower is symbolic of a vital aspect of the *self-creating and self-manifesting agency;* he appears demonic, but that is a part of life. It seems tragic to us that we must experience this "Behemoth" as a natural and necessary part of our human nature, but this is our task and when we accept it as such the sense of tragedy fades. The power represented by the stone thrower is not absolute but relative, and to the degree that we experience this relativity we know our finiteness and our dignity. Our acceptance of the task is the decisive criterion; it is the way to the psyche's wholeness, to the realization of the ontogenetic purpose, not only in ourselves as individuals, but in humanity itself in all its potential grandeur.

Plate 11: March 5, 1956

Joan said about this drawing, "These people are all dead." The experience here depicted and Joan's particular suffering in this instance has been referred to as an *abaissement du niveau mental.* The level upon which the psyche is active has dropped toward a state of seeming nothingness, mere biological existence with little or no awareness of the intrinsically human or of possible access to creative energies. This is the true existential "nothingness"—*the nothingness of anonymity.*

When Joan was asked whether she felt she had ever been alive, her only answer was a look compounded of hope and doubt. She doubted because she had always lived under the threat of Apsu's plotting; she had had no other experience of those transpersonal forces within herself for which Apsu stands as archetype; for which, on the personal level, her own father stood as fact. Her father loomed in the foreground of her view of existence, and it was only at this stage and by means of her drawings that she could begin to see around and behind him, so to speak, and reduce him

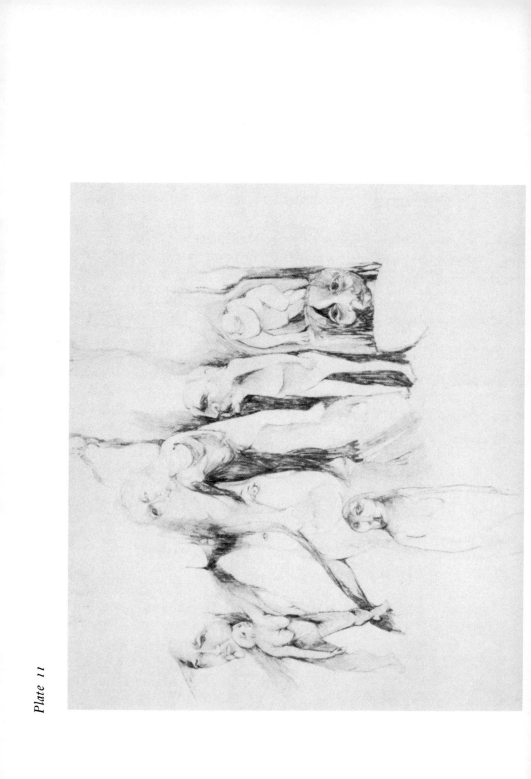

Plate 11

Plate 12

to proper human scale in a world that was truly herself. She had hope because the developing psychotherapeutic situation promised to give her a new and steady angle from which to view her world.

Plate 12: March 7, 1956

Joan called this drawing "The Mountain." There is simultaneous ascent and descent, like the ascent-descent to the realm of the mothers in Goethe's *Faust* ("Steig hinab, ich könnt auch sagen, steige.").

Plates 13–17: April 10 and 25, 1956

Like "The Mountain," these five drawings are additional views of the realm of the inertia and they show a new aspect of it. Its asmosphere and the forces at work within it are more than Joan's, more than personal and private. (Remember that the Babylonian poets imagined man to be created from Kingu's blood, and that the significant thing about him was his dependence on the parental image for his own sense of himself.) Just as the child's body is a continuation and extension of the bodies and the physical heritage of the parents, so the child's psyche is in a very real sense a continuum of the parents' psyches. The shadow of the parents, what is undeveloped and undifferentiated in them, is handed down to the child. ("The fathers have eaten a sour grape and the children's teeth are set on edge.") This is one of the ways by which the psyche evolves, pursuing through the individual an onto-genetic goal for all humanity. The great question is always what the individual will do with the *whole* of his inheritance. Joan's parents of course had their own fears, anxieties, frustrations, denials and dreams; their misunderstanding of their daughter and of her gifts is a sign of their misunderstanding of themselves. At this stage Joan was contained in the abode of her parents, like the gods in the abode of Apsu and Tiamat; she lay in their shadow, breathing its air. Referring to Plate 15, she wrote in her diary, "I lived in hell and breathed the air of breath"—the breath of her parents. Their shadow, coupled in these drawings with her own, prevented her from seeing them as father and mother, as separate and finite human beings; to her, at this point, they were joined together in a single hateful unity. There is no question of sin, guilt or blame on the parents' part; they are not villains; they are simply human

Plate 13

beings, and what we are talking about is the human condition.

> Master, who did sin, this man, or his parents, that
> he was born blind?
> Jesus answered, Neither hath this man sinned, nor
> his parents: but that the works of God should be made
> manifest in him.

John 9:2–3

Plate 14

In Plate 16, she draws herself as attached to the father's head (suggestive of Athene who sprang from the head of Zeus); in Plate 17, she is contained within the womb of the mother. It is of considerable significance that she experiences *both* the father- and mother-images within the inner world as forces of creativity of *equal value.*

During the time these drawings were made, Joan wrote in her diary:

"I remember being me and being with Joyce [her sister] . . . and our friends were young, and maybe even Joyce was young . . . but I don't know, and I felt as if I had to be strong, and felt like I should never tell Joyce or even me what I felt because it was too soft and like the sky . . . and I was a clown and she laughed . . . and I *was* funny. I was the hardest, most cynical child in the world. I took pleasure from the fact that dogs and children disliked me. I felt three million years old. As I grew older I felt younger.

"I'm made, I'm made of solid stone . . .
hard . . . too brittle to break
I'm made, I'm made of solid stone . . .
of solid, solid stone.
I'm heavy like a rock lying bloodless and cold
I cannot speak or be understood
for people don't understand rocks.
My heart is made of solid stone
And no one knows the difference,
the difference
And no one knows the difference,
the difference . . . or cares."

In reply to a comment about the artistic quality of her drawings, she said:

"Artist, what a laugh, I only ease myself. All prostitutes should be able to draw, all idiots too, all weak disgusting people should be able to draw. I wish I could be eaten alive by vultures. I wish dark monsters could claw at me and pick the dirt from my bones. I want to be picked apart and eaten by the ugliest things alive. I wish I were a prostitute begging for love. I wish I were naked and disgraced. I wish I were in the cool earth. I am not disgusted now, I am disgusting."

Plate 16

Plate 17

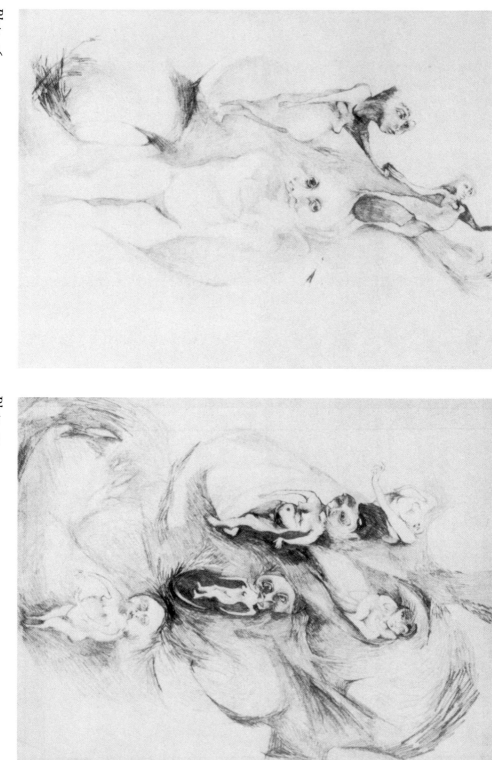

Plates 18 and 19: July 2, 1956

Two months passed, and she executed only these two drawings. On the first (Plate 18) she wrote:

"Mind, you are incorrigible. I was afraid to draw. I don't trust my hand or my mind. They both doubted each other and it was a terrible feeling. I was so conscious of *doing* a drawing. . . . It ruins the only thing that really means anything to me . . . my only way of living."

She withdrew. She could not, at this stage, go on with her remarkable explorations through the medium of her art. She wrote:

"Don't turn around
Don't let these eyes see
Don't look
Don't see.
Twist the mass of yourself inward . . . inward
There you are pure and safe
Ah, sweet safety,
sweet safety.
Your body does not exist.
What importance is it?
Your self exists only for yourself
and there it sees only the light of fear.
This fear exists only for yourself
Therefore it does not exist, you make it so.
How fine,
How very fine
Your fear does not exist even inwardly.
Outwardly you are quite untouchable,
Untouchable,
Ha, Ha,
Nothing can touch me
For I have negated the world
It is only a dream now
Tomorrow I can laugh at it
And although it touches me in a million different ways
and every moment of my most unimportant life
It shall never really touch me
It shall never really touch me.

Plate 19

"When I was young and my friends were gay and youthful, I condemned them with my hatred and my silence. I hated their joviality, their stupid gaiety. . . . I only joined them when I could belittle, when I could mock, when I could openly hate . . . not only them but myself. What a fool I am for writing on this paper now . . . if only the realization of what I say would not frighten me . . . and make me feel so hopelessly lost to everyone."

But something very vital took place during this period of withdrawal, and her next drawing shows it.

Plate 20: July 5, 1956

Choice—the human prerogative, the experience of which is symbolized with such grandeur in the action of the *Akedah*—becomes a possibility for Joan with this picture.

"If only the realization of what I say would not frighten me."

She was afraid of choice itself. She could not, of course, imagine a state of being in which she would be free of the brutal forces that gripped her, a state in which she would begin to *feel* and to act out of that feeling independently, as herself. The Unknown, unimaginable, filled her with fear. If she could *consciously* have chosen, her choice would no doubt have been in favor of the known, the imprisonment; but the forces of her psyche had already taken a different course.

"It shall never really touch me."

In spite of her fear and this determination never to be touched, it happened that she was touched, and the event is revealed here. She did not rationally grasp it or really know of it; it happened in the primal realm, like revelation, and she renders it in terms of a cosmic event. The sky seems to have split; lightning strikes down. The three figures, still brutal, destructive and full of negativity, are nevertheless caught up in attitudes of bewilderment and awe. The child, with an animal's head, clings to the mother. The birth of feeling seems to have taken place and to be rendered here.

Revelation is never anything but promise until it is manifested in action, and the same is true of choice. This drawing is symbolic of something decisive that has happened in the primal realm; if it had not happened, Joan would have been lost to the brutal forces of her inner world. As a symbol, the drawing implies

Plate 20

Plate 21

the possibility that the same event may now take place in consciousness. It is now possible that Joan may begin to feel in her own way, to react out of her own individuality, to breathe a different air. She may *choose*—and it is exactly this, the possibility of choice, that is necessary if the autonomous, deterministic character of the unconscious is to be transformed and the way opened for the experience of individuality and of the Self.

Plate 21

The promise of feeling—that is, to be able to know what she herself really prefers and thus to be able to choose—sounds in a remark Joan made about this drawing: "I *hate* the face looking up, but I *love* the girl that sees nothing."

Plate 22: July 7, 1956

About this picture Joan wrote, "The stones have blended together to become the stalks of growing things."

The quickening of the stones takes place in the presence of a most significant figure: the *hermaphrodite,* the woman with many breasts and with a penis, who in the drawing appears isolated from all the other chaotic events. The hermaphrodite is a collective symbol found in all cultures, and it stands for a *natural activity* of the psyche, an insistent urge toward structure and form through which opposed energies and inertias are reconciled. "The symbol of the hermaphrodite in its functional significance does not point backwards but forward toward a goal which is not yet reached."[91] It is, therefore, an archetypal symbol for *what is* and for what *may be* within the psyche, for it points toward creativity.

The New Birth

Here is born the Empress of all honour/
The philosophers name her their daughter.
She multiplies/bears children ever again/
They are incorruptibly pure and without any stain. . . .
And never did I become a mother/
Until the time I was born another. . . .
Then it was that I first knew my son/
And we two came together as one.

208

There I was made pregnant by him and gave birth
Upon a barren stretch of earth.
I became a mother yet remained a maid/
And in my nature was established.
Therefore my son was also my father/
As God ordained in accordance with nature.
I bore the mother who gave me birth;
Through me she was born again upon earth.[92]

The multiple paradoxes of these lines, written in the six-teenth century, are resolved the moment one sees that what is being talked about is the creativity of the human psyche. The poet makes use of metaphors of biological productivity to de-scribe the very opposite: the flesh must necessarily be created by the flesh, but the psyche is self-creative, a true union of opposites that sustains itself out of its relation with Being. This is one of the deepest insights into his nature that man has achieved, and it finds its purest expression in the symbol of Christ as hermaphrodite (Plate 23). In this image of Him who was God-Man, the primal waters, once mingled, then divided by the Word, are reunited in pure awareness; male and female, Yin and Yang are joined in a *unio oppositorum* that is a vision not only of the human experience of the Divine but also of human wholeness in its fullest realization, the ontogenetic purpose of the psyche having been fully achieved.*

On the deeply personal level, the symbol of the woman with a penis had another significance for Joan. It was a fact that in her pathological state she experienced her mother and father not as individual human beings but as one, locked together as a unity. This "unity," the diametric opposite of the symbolic hermaphro-

---

* "The Church symbolism of *sponsus* and *sponsa* leads to a mystic union of the two, i.e., to the *anima Christi* which lives in the *corpus mysticum* of the Church. This unity underlies the idea of Christ's androgyny, which mediaeval alchemy exploited for its own ends. The much older figure of the Hermaphroditus, whose outward aspect probably derives from a Cyprian *Venus barbata,* encountered in the Eastern Church the already extant idea of the androgynous Christ, which is no doubt connected with the Platonic conception of the bisexual First Man, for Christ is ultimately the Anthropos." C. G. Jung, *The Practice of Psychotherapy,* p. 306.

Plate 23. Christ as the Hermaphrodite

dite, so filled the spaces of her inner world that she could see and feel little else. But here, still face to face with this pathological reality, she draws what coexists with it. With the appearance of the hermaphrodite, the psyche reveals the resources it has for its own cure. The hermaphrodite takes a central position, and a new phase of Joan's art begins. The imagination drops its chains, there is a hint of rhythm and form, and gradually she speaks in a different way about her work.

Plate 24: July 8, 1956

"There are endless growls."

Despite the "growls," there is evident a kind of determination to find order in the chaos.

Plate 25: July 9, 1956

"I am getting annoyed. The damned figures keep changing position."

The figures, human and animal and some forms of vegetation, seem to emanate, as it were, from a devil's head, or an animal's—Behemoth's—achieving in the surge of energy a semblance of form. It is the primal source asserting itself, a kind of visualization of the meaning of the dream quoted on page 46: The Word having been referred back to the animal, this is what takes place. A most important figure appears, and its position relative to the devil's head is most meaningful: it is the ram or goat to the right of the center of the drawing.

Plate 26

"A new kind of unhappiness I feel. It is not black and painful, and yet it is worse than before." She begins really to feel, as an individual, those experiences of human nature that before she had only dimly apprehended.

Plate 27: July 19, 1956

"There is no peace. A large and aged man weighs the grains of time within my head. Unknown women appear."

The "large, aged man" is the large *female* figure at the center of the drawing. Joan is unconsciously referring to the hermaphrodite.

At this time she wrote in her diary:

"When I left your office on Friday there was something I remembered after it was too late, and it is very important to me. Remember I told you once that I was impressed by a Van Gogh painting. It seemed to me that there was a force at the back of the painting which pulled everything into an intense order giving it form. I said that that was what I was beginning to experience myself. On Friday in drawing class I painted a figure. I had to fight with the shapes, they all wanted to go back because this force was pulling so hard. I did not want them to. I felt that I would be left with a lot of oversimplified boulders. I also felt that perhaps this force was my unconscious itself, or my mother. I must add that the part of me that fights this force is very strong too. In this drawing many of the forms seem to rest on a plane, the space behind this plane goes into the distance. The lines always form a triangular shape. This drawing itself seems to be a sort of dead-end valley, surrounded by mountains, or a vagina. This is considering the whole drawing."

Writing this, she knew very well what she was saying on one level, but not at all what she was saying on another, deeper one. She knew nothing about the symbols and mythological motifs discussed at such length in this book; certainly she had no inkling of the significance of the archetypes they represent. Yet in her remark that "the lines always form a triangular shape" she unconsciously expressed her direct experience of the activity of an archetype. And she had felt the "force" at the back of the picture that gives it form. This made it possible to begin to speak to her about the fundamental concepts set down here; specifically, at this stage, to speak of the masculine and feminine archetypes as agents of motivation and action within the psyche. But this does not mean that she was given answers to the questions she asked herself; any answer would have been an intellectual imposition and no help at all, only a hindrance to the psyche that had already proved itself capable of progress toward its own cure.

Plate 27

Plate 28

"Now, when I put people in atmospheres it is always in valleys and mountains. Femininity itself might be my shell. I am afraid of razors. I always feel myself cutting off my arm, or head, or finger. I gave myself security before; encouraging to know it does not exist."

This remark makes it clear that Joan is becoming aware of her containment; at the same time she is cynical in her fear of approaching any degree of freedom. The blades of grass reappear on this drawing.

Plates 29–33

She kept at her drawing, but her inertia was great and dead set against the new hopeful change that came with the appearance of the hermaphrodite.

"I think I am afraid that if I am real things will mean more to me and I will be ruined. How easy it is to say that nothing exists in the world. . . . I am an animal with no understanding except a vague confusion. . . . I see nothing . . . I do not want to be seen. I am strong. I can drop a flood bomb and singe your speaking shapes. If you want to die, keep knowing me. I don't want to have any more contacts with human beings . . . never, never, never. I don't want them to kill me."

"I hate to draw now. I am too stuck. I have no feeling in me now but death, and I am sick and tired of it. I don't want to draw it anymore. Oh, shut your mouth, you cold dead fish, and I know what I am saying now: that, sir, is to say sometimes I just felt things, and when I spoke them I felt guilty, but now I understand and know I am a cold dead fish. Thank you, dearie, for the pretty justification."

The primal inertia, the true adversary, is now out in the open. She experiences it in "hating" to draw and in her fear. "I am afraid that if I am real . . ." Speaking here out of the depth of her suffering, doesn't she also speak for her century? Her very potentialities for growth seem to her a threat of annihilation. She is afraid that if she is real, all she knew of herself before, no matter how pale and partial a summation it was, will be destroyed. She cannot see that what is really threatened is her identification with the parental psyche and her own inertia; that what is *not* threatened, what is in fact promised, is that *Existence* which is individual and, ultimately, invulnerable. Her fear of cutting off her arms or head or fingers is a direct manifestation of the inertia that determinedly thwarts the development of relations with the forces of her inner world and simultaneously creates her anxieties.

During this phase, quite understandably, she offered great resistance to the psychotherapeutic situation.

Plate 30

Plate 31

Plate 32

Plate 33

Plate 34: Sept. 15, 1956

"I feel there is something keeping me from drawing."

Joan had never been able to be objective about her work—objective in the sense that the finished drawing had a meaning for her in terms of her own individuality. Each drawing was a "happening" to which she had no conscious committment. Remember her remark about Plate 18: "I was so conscious of doing a drawing . . . I hated that. It ruins the only thing that means anything to me . . . my only way of living." There is a kind of spectrum of meaning here, and the shadings are very important. Any artist hates being "conscious" of working, if "conscious" means having the sense of manipulating his material instead of participating with it in a living dynamic process. The condition he strives for (and, in the final analysis, it *is* what means most to him; it *is* his only way of *living*) is certainly not to be defined by anyone other than himself, but for all artists it is evidently a condition in which the line between objective and subjective, willing instrument and creative agent, conscious and unconscious is so finely drawn as to render these words meaningless. The condition, that is, is met when the artist, as individual, finds himself truly situated at that focal point where the inner and outer orders of experience lose their separateness and opposition. What Joan meant by her remark is far down the scale from this. To be *unconscious* had been her only way of living. She wanted her art simply to happen; her ideal working condition was one in which human individuality did not really exist and the drawing simply drew itself.

But now, as she is able consciously to write that "something" is keeping her from drawing, there is an implication of consciousness of herself *in relation* with her drawing. She was asked whether she could explain what was happening in Plate 34 and what it meant to her. She wrote in answer:

"The figure in the middle with the arms crossed is new. The figure does not stand freely but is only emerging and stands on a spot where the ground has split, in a hole in the ground which can take any direction. To the right of this figure is a path leading down to it. The figure close to it is anxious, very female, and rather feeble. She can do nothing. She seems not even to understand. There is a figure which although on the same path looks in the other direction. She is unhappy and can see nothing . . . perhaps she does see something, but I don't know what it is. She is a skeptic, she is frightened. Next to her is another female. This one takes rather large strides in the direction of the newcomer. She comes from far back and is gentle with the one who sees her own dreams. Next to her is the one who is too frightened and too defensive to have any personality of her own or any strength or any thoughts. Just below her is the mad one. She wants only to escape, and refuses all thought. She is gay, she is carefree. She is stuck. To the left of the newcomer are two ugly females. The large one sleepy-eyed is the woman who keeps slime upon the floor. She has no personality but sleeps, and her friend whose left arm reaches backward has none either. The light has made her angry. She knows nothing but anger and hate. The large female encloses all with her arm . . . but all would be enclosed anyhow in spite of her arm. Three figures walk within the same body, one is unhappily walking off the page or into the arms of the largest women. The middle one can be seen in two ways, either protecting the other from the newcomer and the people in the path, holding her, pushing her into the direction in which she is going (perhaps against the other's will) or else—looking at the people in the lower level, which in this case is consciousness. She is skeptical of consciousness, as she is skeptical of the newcomer. She looks very strong and yet she trusts nothing, yet she does care about the figure she is pushing. The third part is rather a clown. She doesn't want to go along with the others but she must, and so she waves sadly goodbye, or is she trying to get the newcomer's attention? . . . at any rate she is not seen. On the lower level to the left is a rather dreamy-eyed female. A child has grown within her. One figure next to her is trying to escape, but part of it attacks it, so that it will not shut its eyes to what part it must play (and yet if it does it will be of no use whatsoever. I wonder if it isn't trying to bring it back to consciousness). Next, a figure which looks to another on its knees, is trying to tell the other something but he is so frightened (I think he is only trying to let him know he is alive and not to tell him anything). Between them a catlike woman revels in herself. She is looking out."

This long discussion of a single picture was a vital step forward for Joan. What she has written is certainly not a rational

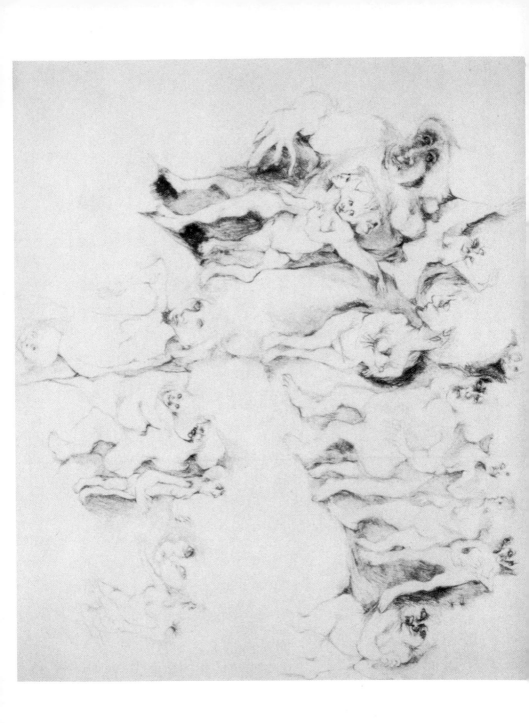

critique; it is contemplative. She shows herself capable of a withdrawal drastically different from that other that was pathological and a mode of death. One withdraws into contemplation in order to be engaged, and she does this here; she takes the picture with her, considers the feelings of the figures she has drawn and, by doing so, begins a tentative approach to evaluation of her own feelings.

Plate 35: Oct. 12, 1956

"Perhaps masculinity is only an idea and there are parts of me which I think are masculine, or maybe they are, but they don't have to remain that way or disappear. How can forms come so easy to me? What is the connection between ideas and the senses? Hah, who gives a damn?"

Sir Herbert Read has made a statement that seems to me to answer Joan's question:

> I am convinced that in the deeper layers of the unconscious there is a formative principle at work, moulding some primordial material of the psyche into icons. I prefer to call them icons rather than symbols, because the word symbol is ambiguous. An icon is an image wrought out of the *materia primordialis* of the unconscious and its purpose is to provide an objective correlative—an object with apprehensible form and color—*that answers to an unconscious need.* [My italics][93]

Joan's drawings would seem, in turn, to add weight to this profound statement. The forms that come to her with such puzzling ease are, by the above definition, *icons* molded out of the primordial materials of the psyche. The essential "connection" between ideas and the senses, the agents of meaning, is, I suggest, human individuality itself. Throughout Joan's work this is what has been tragically lacking; this has been the desperate unconscious need that, under the impetus of the formative principles of the psyche, has brought the pictures into being. As objective correlatives, they answer the *need* in that they are the attempts of an intrinsic individuality to establish relations with those forces that have thwarted its growth—attempts, that is, to establish personality.

Plate 35

Plate 36

The success of these attempts begins to be evident. In the early drawings (see, for example, Plate 10), all one sees are the first views of the primal realm: *chaos in simultaneity.* Energy manifests itself mindlessly in outpourings of turbulent forms; there is no source, no humanity, no human connection. As some sense of form in the drawing as a whole (beginning with Plate 25) becomes evident, there is also a suggestion of *source;* the creative surge seems to pour from the devil's (or animal's) head. In Plate 35 Joan draws a monstrous but *human* figure, female, *herself,* from whose head the events seem to have surged. The human begins to take its place, its unique situation, in relation with the enormous forces of creativity. She begins to have some dim sense of herself as a being distinct within the order of experience these forces represent.

In her remarks about this picture, quoted above, Joan makes an extraordinary statement—she had no way of knowing *how* extraordinary or how right. She says that those parts of her that are "masculine" do not "have to remain that way or disappear." I have already pointed out that in her pathological state she experienced the father- and mother-images in the inner world as equal in value and of equal force, though locked together in a unity. Here, in reference to creativity itself, she questions the concept of the "masculinity" of certain forces of her being and gives herself an answer that is precisely right. What we are accustomed to call the "male" and "female" aspects of the psyche are by no means to be taken as fixed and definable forces, capable by their nature of being circumscribed by intellections based on biological and essentially social observations. Any talk of "male" and "female" principles within the psyche must be taken as at best a feeble attempt to define the indefinable; as rationalistic and mechanistic and having very little to do with the truth of things. The human psyche is by nature creative; it *becomes* creative, its energetic potential is fulfilled, when the *individual* within it emerges and is active in relation with both the inner and outer orders of experience. In this light, discussion of "male" and "female" principles within the psyche is off the point, unless one is aware that what is being referred to is a single force that the individual experiences by qualities which may lend themselves to description in terms of the biological equation. And it depends on the individual as to whether or not, through his experience, the *single* force becomes *dual,* specifically masculine or feminine and therefore, as it were, askew. The individual expresses himself *as he is,* certainly; but no question is of less significance than that of masculinity or femininity when the individual, whether scientist or artist, is in the midst of the creative process. The closer he comes to the act itself, the more all the forces of his being are equalized, focused, refined to the exact center that is the creation itself. The question becomes significant only when what we call "male" and "female" qualities and attributes are fixed *opinions,* essentially moods, even postures, and therefore against the truth of our nature, destructive, counter to creativity.

Plate 36

The process by which the inner world slowly becomes an objective reality continues. There is a lapse here, a fall back and away from the relative height Joan achieved in Plate 35; but this is usual in the psychotherapeutic relationship. There are highs and lows, so to speak, sudden lights and long periods of darkness, as long as the pagan round is not broken. But even here some of the figures are drawn in attitudes of urgency, reaching up out of the dark of containment. And with the next picture a dramatic event takes place.

Plate 37: Dec. 8, 1956

From the point of view of the psychotherapist, this drawing secures all Joan has accomplished up to now and therefore marks the turning point from schizophrenia to neurosis. The sense of imprisonment, of containment within the dark realms of the psyche, is gone. As a drawing, it is open. The figures are still, as though there has been a sudden cessation of turbulence in the inner landscape. The formative principle may be said to reveal its own ends and purposes here. Until this happened, nothing was secure. Joan wrote on the back of this drawing a single word "Foo!"—an onomatopoetic expression of her great sense of relief. It is the sigh that comes with significant achievement, with having taken a step, albeit unconsciously, out of the prison where she had always lived.

The ram appears again in this drawing—the black figure left of center.

Plate 37

Plate 38

The achievement was real; but again this does not mean that all thereafter was changed for Joan. The break-through had been a long time in coming and its effects will be a long time in being felt. But *long* and *short, fast* and *slow* are meaningless terms where the psyche is concerned. Its processes simply are not measurable, for the hub of all its workings is the instant, what T. S. Eliot has called "the still point of the turning world."[94]

During this period Joan's fears overtake her again, she gives way to inertia, and there is the same *abaissement du niveau mental* as was evident in Plate 11; the figures here are very like those others who were "all dead." Now, however, the crowd of figures is reduced to three, and the energy is concentrated and focused in such a way as to reveal their true nature. In this drawing of herself in relation with mother and father, Joan unconsciously reveals part of the reason why she has "felt dead"; she approaches an insight into the "parental complex" within her that has hampered her growth. But the surest evidence of the psyche's progress toward its own cure is that now she holds in her hands the blades of grass that earlier grew at the feet of the archetype (Plate 10). She is still caught between the mother- and father-images, but in that situation she holds at last the symbol of her own individual existence.

The Sumerian *Epic of Gilgamish* is significant here:

What shall I give thee [as gift] wherewith to return/to
    thy country?
Gilgamish, I will reveal thee a hidden matter . . . I'll
    tell thee:
There is a plant like a thorn with its root [?] deep down/
    in the ocean,
Like unto those of the briar [in sooth] its prickles will/
    scratch thee,
[Yet] if thy hand reach this plant, thou'lt surely find/
    life [everlasting].*
[Then], when Gilgamish heard this, he loosen'd [?]
    his/girdle about him,
Bound heavy stones on his feet, which dragg'd him
    down to/the sea-deeps,

* See Part I, page 85.

Plate 38

Found he the plant; as he seized on the plant, (lo), its/
prickles did scratch him.

Though he had descended to the primal depths to seize this
"plant of great wonder . . . whereby a man may attain his desire,"
when he returned to the shore and broke his fast and rested,

Gilgamish spied out a pool of cool water, [and] therein/
descending
Bathed in the water. [But here was] a serpent who
snuff'd/the plant's fragrance,
Darted he up from the water [?], and snatched the
plant/uttering malison
As he drew back.[95]

Plates 39–42: March 1 and 9, 1957

When Joan first descended into the primal realm, she, like
Gilgamish, encountered its blind impersonal forces. Now, unlike
him, she holds the "plant of great wonder" in her hand, she does
not let go of it; and as though by virtue of this fact, she approaches
a view of herself. The parental images and the parental shadow
give way as she comes face to face with an aspect of her own most
personal shadow. In Plate 39, she draws for the first time since her
treatment began an isolated figure, a jeering mocking creature, an
icon in which is distilled the feelings and actions of the child she
used to be. It is a direct look at an aspect of her own identity, and
it opens the way for a wider and deeper look. In Plates 40 and 41,
she draws herself in total isolation. There is a suggestion of unlimited space around her, unlimited freedom to move, but the
view is bleak. It is not only her own but humanity's essential predicament: finite, but somehow part of the infinite; ultimately
alone by virtue of being unique, but somehow, at every instant, a
part of Being. Lack of awareness of the latter is what makes the
view so bleak. This experience of her own and of the human predicament was necessary for Joan's future as a person and as an
artist.

In Plate 43, the same lonely figure turns to watch herself
being helped, carried on an old man's back.

Plate 39

Plate 41

Plate 43

Plates 43 and 44

The sense of openness and potential freedom persists, but neither here nor in the preceding drawings is there any focal action in specific space and time; there is no sense of what is so necessary to the work of art—the certainty that the instant has been seized and rendered with formal intent. Everything is simultaneous; things are simply happening. The figures (images of herself as she sees herself) are simply there, suspended in time, lacking dynamic interrelation with the space they occupy. But there are lines, paths, delineations along which action might take place—signs, it would seem, pointing to the possibility of a relationship with the instant. Until the individual achieves a relationship with the instant, with the immediate vivid interplay of both orders of experience, the springs of creativity cannot be stirred into play.

On the back of Plate 44, Joan wrote, significantly: "I run out of people."

She remains in the phase of reflection. The process of differentiation, by which the intrinsic individuality emerges into dynamic relations with the "other," has not been accomplished.

Plates 45 and 46

For the first time during the psychotherapeutic process, Joan uses color, giving dramatic emphasis to the experiences she has had of the unsuspected dimensions of her inner world. On the back of Plate 45 she wrote:

"I am here where my feet lay watching the roads, the endless roads, the infinite number of roads. The direction each one takes, the roads that can never really branch out anywhere because they continually come back to the central stream. These, these, so long, so long . . . they cover vast areas of space, and like the dry bones of a finished fish each branch can only go so far. And it does. Each branch goes so far and ends, but the main branch continues on and on. Futility created for and with the grabbing hands of the weak. And love is the word which exists and cannot exist . . . for *it is an unrealized idea,* but these bony paths, they cannot go that far. They will not go that far. My mind is the conspirator. The conspirator to the ends, the infinite ends. It follows each path anew yearning and desparing. . . . Or, or, or is it energy which starts these paths, and do they continue, do they continue unseen by me? Are they covered by the fullness of the hills? Are they low on the ground and lost in the hilly landscape? [My italics]

"And the mountains, the mountains which are formed by the roads, the mountains which are the roads, roads lost. Can a road form a barrier to another road? The mountains which are the roads form plains. High and rocky and inhuman, yet they are plains . . . plains of many colors and of many roads.

"The people are in the sea and the sea forms stones, separates the land. As do too many roads which cross each other."

With reference to Plate 46, she wrote, "There are destructive roads and the roads of dishonesty." Her statement is meaningful far beyond her private situation. The roads are inevitably destructive for all of us, and dishonest, as long as love is "an unrealized idea."

Plate 45 (facing)

Plate 46 (overleaf)

Plates 47–49: April 5, 1957

With these three drawings Joan adds significantly to her achievement. Out of her first experience of herself as a finite and solitary being, the hermaphrodite reappears (Plate 47) and is immediately differentiated into the primal female (Plate 48) and the primal male archetypes (Plate 49). This act of differentiation is of the greatest importance: the waters must be divided, the dualities must be experienced by the emergent individuality before that unity and wholeness that is creative can ever be achieved. Personality is established in the midst of the multiplicity and oppositions of things, but on the basis of it one may come eventually to an awareness of their harmony and oneness.

Joan referred to the bird perched on the shoulder of the female archetype as a pelican. It is an old, familiar symbol, dense in its meanings. Its name comes from the Greek *pelekon,* a hatchet, owing to the shape of the beak, and on one level it is symbolic of the destructive element of the mother. On another, higher level, in heraldry, the pelican was pictured feeding its young with blood from its own breast and was seen as allegorical of Christ. According to a Christian legend, the pelican kills her young by beating them to death with her wings, but after three days the mother opens her side and revives them with her own blood, and thus she reaffirms the death and rebirth of Christ.[96]

In Plate 49, Joan draws what she calls "the party guest." He is the male archetype bearing fire, symbolic of the coming of light, as the pelican is symbolic of the coming of love.

Plate 47

Plate 49

Plates 50 and 51: June 29, 1957

Throughout the two years of her treatment discussed here and during all the time since, Joan has returned again and again to her abiding problem: the child-parent relationship. Psychotherapy could never pretend to be able to *solve* this problem for her or to rid her of it. The best to be hoped for (and this is all the psychotherapist can hope for any patient) is to make her able to come to terms with it; not simply to endure it but to relate with it in such a way that the problem itself becomes a source of creative energy. Here, following the differentiation of the hermaphrodite, she takes another look at the situation between parent and child and sees it in a truer and more human light. She is no longer wholly identified with the parental psyche: the parents are separated one from the other, no longer a "unity," and the child, though related with them, is apart and distinctly other. She wrote on the back of Plate 50:

"I am not afraid that I *am* my mother anymore. I am afraid that I *think* I am my mother. . . . Is seeing things as ideas enough to understand, or must understanding come from seeing in reality? I mean something more than reality. I expect to pull myself into different realities, to stay there and expect something to dawn on me because I am there."

Her experience of the creative forces of the inner world began with the appearance of the hermaphrodite in Plate 22; it was expressed in Plate 25, where the devil's or animal's head appears as source; again in Plate 35 and in her very important remark about the "masculine" in her, which need not stay that way. Now, having directly confronted the male and female archetypes and having freed herself to a degree from her identification with the parental images, she returns in her remarks to the experience of the creative force and, in effect, questions the "femininity" of it. She senses that there are "different realities" to be experienced and she expects to pull herself into them—to pull herself, in other words, into a state in which she may apprehend the qualities of the creative force directly, in its unity, neither male nor female nor anything but itself. I am certain she is not alone in this experience; it is, I suggest, the true motive and impetus of the most serious modern art.

245

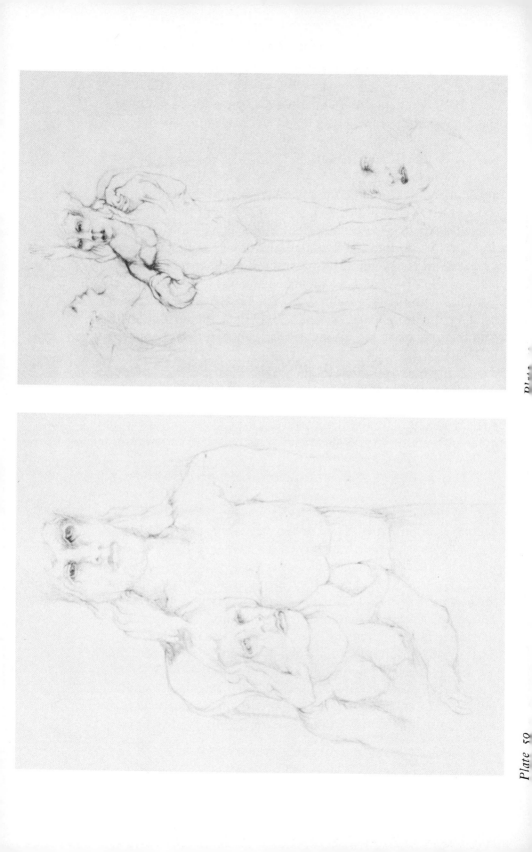

Plate 59

It is important to note that in Plate 50 Joan draws the parents standing together and herself separate from them, seeming to glance back toward them. In Plate 51 she is suddenly able to render the mother and child with a kind of serenity of feeling.

Plates 52–57: July 3 to October 25, 1957

"I can't think, this is no good . . . fear. I don't believe I am myself. I hate this and am tired and my eyes may be anywhere. I can't be alone, because of that I get angry."

Nevertheless, she draws the solitary figure, elaborating the fact that she does not allow herself to be by herself. Each single figure is like a character study, as though of a face she had really seen. Remote as sages, having more and more a look of strange genius, they are renderings of the male archetype—further explorations of the event of differentiation that was revealed by Plates 47, 48 and 49. When she drew these pictures Joan was just twenty-one years old.

At this period, the problem of transference to the psychotherapist and the problem of her father became acute.

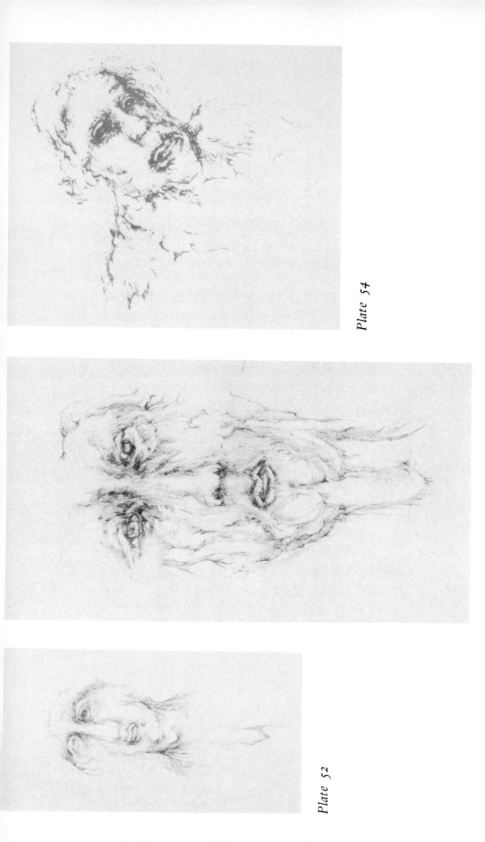

Plate 54

Plate 53

Plate 52

Plate 56

Plate 57

Plate 58

"Oh boy . . . but how deep is your vision now? A good thing not to take things I see for granted. Truly, if this is as it seems, art is the only life."

Thus Joan answers her question: it is not enough to "see things as ideas"; understanding can only come from "seeing in reality." Or, to put it another way, it is again the problem of Job, who had heard with the hearing of his ears "but now mine eye seeth thee." The human being must, in his individuality, be related with the instant; otherwise he lacks distinctness within the orders of experience and, clear though his vision may seem to him to be, the "things" he sees will not appear to him in their purity and their true identity, for they will bear the burden of the dark forces of his inner world, which are inevitably projected upon them.

Plate 59

The scrawl across this drawing reads: "Painting is too difficult. Life stinks. I am being destructive."

Just as Joan returns again and again to the problem of the child-parent relationship, so she returns also to the problem of faith and hope that always besets the artist. Art may well be the "only life" for her, but the certainty of it must be fought for in an endless series of battles; each picture, each work is the first; earlier successes are of next to no comfort; from start to finish, failure is the likelier outcome. Joan is not yet strong enough to take the daily risk of failure. Despair overtakes her, painting becomes too difficult, and life stinks.

On the back of this drawing she wrote, "This is an illustration for parts or words of a story. I feel this is a bad thing to be doing. It is cowardly. This is exactly what happens when I try to paint. I have to do something! But what?"

Plate 58

aønting is too Difficult
(LIFE STINKS)
I am being DISTRUCTIVE

Plate 59

Plate 60: Nov., 1957

"Works of Art," Sir Herbert Read has written, "embody an independent and free development of perceptual experience."[97]

Joan comments on this painting:

"I am doing this, *letting it do what I see,* then something in me wants to start pushing, but that is no good."

To be "conscious" of doing a drawing no longer ruins it for her: it may act, but it is *she* who sees. And she has answered her own question about what to do.

In *The Secret of the Golden Flower* Jung writes:

> We must be willing to let things happen in the psyche. For us, this becomes a real art of which few people know anything. Consciousness is forever interfering, helping, correcting and negating, and never leaving the single growth of the psychic processes in peace. It would be a simple enough thing to do, if only simplicity were not the most difficult of all things. It consists solely of watching objectively the development of any fragment of fantasy.[98]

Plate 61: Nov., 1957

This is the last painting Joan completed in this period of her treatment. She wrote nothing about it; it seems to speak for itself and to reaffirm the promise of independence and freedom.

Plate 60 (facing)

Plate 61 (overleaf)

Conclusion

As I write this (May, 1958) Joan lives with her parents in an atmosphere that is evidently pleasanter than any before. She has developed a sense of order, and a certain generosity and a wish, not necessarily to please, but not to offend. She cares for herself, in other words; she dresses neatly. She has a part-time job and earns enough to buy her art supplies, and she draws and paints regularly. Her experience of psychotherapy did not stop or thwart or even threaten the creative process; rather, it had the opposite effect. She has made great progress toward the establishment of that means of relation with both orders of experience which we have called *personality*. On the one hand, she is capable of relationships with young men of her own age; on the other, she continues to develop through her art her relationships with the forces of her own inner world. She will always, of course, have her ups and downs, crises of belief and hope, and, to some degree, of inertia and despair; but it is her task to come to terms with them, since they are natural to her human condition, are her prerogative as an artist, one might say, and her privilege.

The whole course of her treatment was and continues to be governed by the fact that she is an artist; and that it is primarily through her art that the psyche reveals itself. This explains why there has been no mention of her dreams: they were of very little help. From the beginning Joan so lacked any relation with the forces at work within her that, in effect, she lives her dreams in "reality." The dark forces of her psyche were projected outward and burdened the "things" she saw. The highly complex problem of her father was never touched on by any dream; it had to be faced in dealing with the problem of the transference. The equally complex problem of her mother was projected in her dreams and in everyday life into a relationship with a girl friend, and so it had to be met indirectly. It was in her drawings, day by day, that the truth of Joan's situation came to light and it was through them that the psyche brought about its own cure.

What made this possible was the kind of psychotherapeutic situation in which Joan found herself. The psychotherapist was not an observer-predictor; he was an observer-participant. There were no doctrines, she was never instructed, and there was therefore no question on her part of "doctrinal compliance."[99] There was a single fundamental conviction upon which the psychotherapeutic situation rested—that the psyche is a complex of energies and inertias not only potentially harmonious, balanced and whole, but in its ontogenesis actually determined upon the achievement of harmony, balance and wholeness. Free as this conception is of pansexualism, of anthropological constructs such as matriarchates and patriarchates, free of any notion of the human psyche as primarily a musty storeroom of the repressed, forgotten and denied, free of any theorizing that finds the psyche inevitably dominated by social or biological drives, it provides for both therapist and patient the ground for an experience at once scientific, artistic and religious. Because Joan's psyche was left free to express itself in its own terms, it proceeded to work as the self-regulatory and self-creative agency it truly is and, by means of her drawings, pursued its ontogenetic purpose step by step. In the process, it demonstrated that schizophrenia is not necessarily meaningless human chaos. Joan's drawings are not hallucinations; they are views of human reality. As such, as a visible record of the way the psyche follows in its growth, they are unique.

The theme of Joan's work is the great underlying theme of all our mythologies, legends, tales and sacred books. It is also the theme of our nightly dreams. It abides, beyond all others, as the human preoccupation. Whether we are conscious of it or not, our deepest concern is human individuality and the steps by which it emerges to a condition in which, through its creativity, it vibrantly affirms its relationship with Being.

Diverse and inimical though the modes of science, art and religion and even politics may appear to be, struggle though we do under the banner of one or the other, they have a common impetus and at heart share a common motive that render pointless the distinctions we make between them. Whatever our accomplishments in any of these fields of action and learning in the past, present or future, they will all have come into being out of a single source, the human psyche, and out of the determination of that source to achieve its ontogenetic purpose.

But what is even more important: they will have come into being through human beings, through the individual who, in the integrity of his humanity, is able to descend into the primal ground of our origins where the "self-creating and self-manifesting agency" has dominion over the truth of things.

No matter what name we give to our efforts and no matter what attitudes we adopt on the basis of them, they are in the final analysis directed toward a single transcendental end. To the degree that we realize our humanity; to the degree, that is, that we are individuals, unique but freely and intimately related with the world outside and the world within (and they are, in truth, one and the same world), we become aware of being the medium through which that single transcendental end is to be realized. It is through man, through him alone, that Being, when the stones that block the springs of creativity are rolled back, is able to realize itself in all its potential grandeur.

This is the Great Cause. If it fails, it is because the individual fails—in self-knowledge.

Epilogue to the Case of Joan

In the fullest sense of the word this case illustrates the process of dynamic psychiatry. As the author himself states, his role was not that of "observer-predictor"; he was an "observer-participant," and one feels throughout this presentation his sensitive awareness of the struggles going on within the patient's deep emotional life. In the usual type of case presentation, the reader necessarily feels at some distance from the patient. The patient's life history, his course in therapy, and the description of the psychotherapeutic process are all "filtered through," as it were, the therapist himself, leaving us with a sense of being somewhat apart from the patient.

In the case of Joan, however, the reader has a sense of participating directly in the turmoil of her emotional life. This is made possible by means of the extraordinary series of drawings and paintings which form the focal point of this presentation. These productions of the patient are truly remarkable. Yet when the artistic quality of her drawings was mentioned, she replied: "Artist, what a laugh, I only ease myself," indicating the spontaneous nature of her productions. At another time the outcropping of unconscious material in these drawings is indicated by her saying: "I was afraid to draw. I don't trust my hand or my mind. They both doubted each other and it was a terrible feeling. I was so conscious of *doing* a drawing. . . . It ruins the only thing that really means anything to me. . . . My only way of living." Thus, the reader has presented before his eyes a representation, in pictorial form, of the patient's inmost processes. "It was in her drawings day by day that the truth of her situation came to light and it was through them that the psyche brought about its own cure." When this wealth of material is added to by the therapist's own objective narrative and by the patient's interpretive comments about her art, one feels that one has been immersed in the three-dimensional profile of a schizophrenic process itself—and its step-by-step resolution in the direction of health. There is meaning to even the most distorted of these drawings. Each is a view of reality as she sees it at the time.

The great clinical advance made by Joan was, I believe, due to the skill of the therapist in adapting his approach to the unique situation with which he was presented, rather than treating her in a more conventional manner. He points out that there was little or no utilization of dream material; "in effect, she lived her dreams in 'reality'." The therapist continues: "There were no doctrines, she was never instructed, and there was, therefore, no question on her part of 'doctrinal compliance.' There was a single fundamental conviction upon which the situation rested—that the psyche is a complex of energies and inertias not only potentially harmonious, balanced and whole, but actually in its ontogenesis determined upon the achievement of harmony, balance and wholeness." Would that this declaration of faith in the spirit of man were more widespread in the psychiatry of today! Mr. Westman has rendered us a signal service in substantiating his thesis in such a convincing manner.

ROBERT W. LAIDLAW, M.D.

Appendix: Psychological Report

NAME: _____   *Examined:* 11/29/55
AGES: *19 plus and 22 plus*   *Reexamined:* 12/10/58

Tests given: Rorschach; Szondi; Human Figure Drawings.

_____was resistant to examination on both occasions. The first time she was obviously depressed and seeking help. But when asked to draw she complained that she was an art student and what she drew would be just art. As the examination progressed, she became more cooperative. In 1958, however, she was openly annoyed and on guard against revealing herself. When confronted with the Rorschach she complained, "In painting I *avoid* seeing images and making them into things." The last card, X, pleased her, "Lovely colors and lovely shapes . . . satisfying and unsatisfying because it doesn't mean anything . . . it looks like things I used to draw . . . I wonder . . . you see I hate to make this into things."

The change in the Szondi profiles has been slight. It consists of less acceptance of her need for a tender relationship, but a greater acceptance of being an active outgoing person, more social and less basically hostile.

Her Human Figure Drawings were more human in 1958, and the woman was more girlish, less grotesque, more upright and more relaxed, more passive. The boy was less feminine—instead of the broad hips and narrow shoulders which she drew in 1955, the boy in 1958 had broad shoulders, narrow hips and a penis, as opposed to a feminine conformation of the genital region. Both figures were more representative of normal young people rather than grotesque people aged by life.

Due to the clinical setting in which the records were made it was not possible to secure a full inquiry about the Rorschach responses. The examining rooms were needed for another clinic be-

260

fore the inquiry could be completed. Without this inquiry a definitive scoring and the usual profile of scored responses is not valid. However, it can be said with confidence that productiveness dropped from a total of 51 responses in 1955 to 13 in 1958. In 1958 she gave more human than animal responses, whereas this was in reverse in 1955—a clear indication of greater maturity.

The proportion of M to FM is now higher as is also the proportion of W to M, suggesting that her creativity is greater, her goals more realistic. She is less driven to achieve beyond her capacity. The number of popular responses has increased from one to three. The relative number of pure form as well as poor form responses remains about the same. Anxiety and depressive responses have disappeared. However, the record indicates that her relationships to the father figure and to men are still distorted concepts for her. The progress she has made in the past three years is tremendous, but she is still in need of therapy and will be for some years to come.

The best way to picture the difference between the Rorschach records of 1955 and 1958 is to give selected responses in full. The following protocols for cards I, II, III and VIII are therefore presented in full:

1955	1958

I

8″ It looks like 2 angels
(old men) pulling apart a
big . . . an insect . . . huge.

5″ Two horses with wings
(side figures) . . . in a way
it looks like a figure in the
middle with a bathrobe on.

II

3″ This looks like two
animals . . . could be
sheep . . . no . . . not
sheep . . . snouts have
broken away from them
and are pointing at infinity.
At the same time they're
looking at little nymphs over
the other one's head.
(upper red) It's not blood
because they're not
bleeding.
   Inside view of the bodies
are blood vessels. (red in
black) The two little lines
don't mean anything. (Two
small black lines projecting
into center white).

3″ Oh, me. Two people
(either male or female) in
an argument. I don't want to
go into any great length
about these—remember
them from last time.
   If you look at them a
long time you can see
anything you want.
   I might add it's a very
fierce argument—no I
won't—their hands are up.

III

3″ These two men are pulling
apart a big pot. And a
butterfly over the pot
dancing between them.
And two turkeys in the
background talking to each
other and laughing at the
men because they think the
whole thing is very funny.
The butterfly is drawing the
top of the people together.
Pretty ridiculous.

7″ Two people arguing again.
This time over something
funny. (The center is
what they're arguing
over—they're natives and
there is a pot between
them.) Did I get the same
cards last time? The little
red thing in the middle
is nice.

VIII

4″ These look like polar bears crawling up into the air and two other animals whose faces we cannot see. And these two other animals have fused and a sort of crab-like thing has come from this fusion, with its feet sticking up, its hands down in a grabbing way (upside-down). And below, the tails of the two polar bears are attached to this lump of ice (pink). And in front of the lump of ice there are two men looking up at the whole situation with curiosity and a bit of annoyance.

6″ Very nice. Two polar bears climbing. Below are two animals, (just the pink area) which I can't make out, sitting there watching (waiting). It looks like a man in the middle, a very strong man (gray face, blue shoulders). I saw it in a painting yesterday.

In summary, there is no question but that this young adolescent patient has been greatly helped by therapy in spite of the normal expectation to the contrary with this type of case. Three years ago, her drawings reflected remarkably skilful technique of a highly gifted person whose personality was grossly distorted and bordered on the pathological. She was also severely depressed. Now, the distortions are disappearing and the picture is one of a schizoid, not schizophrenic person with a deep neurotic conflict in relation to the male figure. She is more mature and more realistic and has been relieved of her anxiety and depression even though some of her basic asocial and egocentric character traits persist. But surely the patient is more at one with herself.

HELEN THOMPSON, PH. D.
Chief Clinical Psychologist

Notes

INTRODUCTION

1. C. G. Jung, "Über Psychologie," *Wirklichkeit der Seele* (Zurich, Rascher & Cie., 1934), p. 65. To be published in English in C. G. Jung, *Collected Works*, Vol. 10, London, Routledge & Kegan Paul, and New York, Bollingen Foundation, Inc.
2. John Baillie, *Natural Science and the Spiritual Life* (New York, Oxford University Press, 1951), pp. 25–26.
3. *Ibid*, p. 9.
4. The New York *Times*, November 4, 1959, p. 31.
5. J. H. Oldham, "Personal Decision," *Question, A Journal* (London, Hammond & Hammond), Vol. VI, No. 1 (1953), p. 87.

PART ONE

6. *Tao Te Ching*, Chapter 20, as quoted by Chung-Juan Chang, "The Concept of Tao in Chinese Culture," *The Review of Religion* (New York, Columbia University Press), March, 1953, p. 115.
7. A. D. Ritchie, *The Natural History of the Mind* (London, Longman, Green & Co., 1936), p. 279.
8. *Jeremiah*, 31:29.
9. Saint Augustine, *De Quaestionibus Octaginta Tribus*, Q. 46, "De Ideis" (Migne P.L. XL).
10. H. F. Hallett, *Benedict de Spinoza* (London, University of London, The Athlone Press, 1957), p. 13. Also available in an American edition, New York, Essential Books, Inc., 1957.
11. C. G. Jung, "The Spirit of Psychology," in Joseph Campbell, ed., *Papers from the Eranos Yearbooks,* Bollingen Series XXX, 1 (New York, Pantheon Books Inc., 1954), pp. 412–415.
12. Bertrand Russell, *Human Knowledge* (London, Allen & Unwin, 1951), p. 256.
13. Sir Kenneth Clark, *Moments of Vision* (Oxford, Clarendon Press, 1954). Pamphlet.
14. Samuel Taylor Coleridge, *Anima Poetae,* as quoted by Walter Pater in *Appreciations* (New York: The Macmillan Company, 1903), p. 73.
15. Sir Herbert Read, "Originality," *The Sewanee Review,* LXI, 4 (Autumn, 1953), pp. 555–556.

16. C. G. Jung, *The Practice of Psychotherapy, Collected Works,* Vol. 16, Bollingen Series XX (New York, Pantheon Books Inc., 1954), p. 3.

17. Harry Stack Sullivan, *The Psychiatric Interview* (New York, W. W. Norton & Co., 1954), p. 3.

18. The Old Testament gives two different versions of the legend of the golden calf. See Exodus 31:18, 32:15–20, 30–35; and Exodus 32: 1–6, 7–14, 21–29, 33:1–4.

19. Micha Josef bin Gorion, *Die Sagen der Juden,* "Moses" (Frankfurt am Main, Rütten & Löning, 1926), p. 257.

20. *Ibid,* p. 260.

21. *Ibid,* p. 185.

22. *Der Babylonische Talmud,* Sota I, Fol. 13, a., translated by Lazarus Golschmidt (Berlin, Jüdischer Verlag, 1932), Vol. VI., p. 51ff.

23. Micha Josef bin Gorion, *op. cit.,* p. 265.

24. Numbers 20:12 and Deuteronomy 34:4–5.

25. Louis Ginzberg, *The Legends of the Jews* (Philadelphia, The Jewish Publication Society, 1925), Vol. III, pp. 319–320.

26. *Midrash Rabbah,* translated under the editorship of Dr. H. Freedman and Maurice Simon (London, Soncino Press, 1939), Vol. III, "Exodus," p. 60.

27. II Kings 18:4.

28. This is not to say that science might not, perhaps, at some future date make it possible for others to control our dreams for us. Though, certainly, this is not the subject under discussion here, the reader might be interested to look into recent works which report research into the structure and mechanics of the brain. See especially Max Rinkel and Herman C. B. Deuber, eds., *Chemical Aspects of Psychosis* (New York, McDowell, Obolensky, 1958) and Wilder Penfield writing in *Neurological Basis of Behaviour* (Boston, Little, Brown & Co., 1958).

PART TWO

29. A. Heidel, *The Babylonian Genesis* (Chicago, The University of Chicago Press, 1954), p. 67.

30. *Ibid,* p. 68.

31. Heinrich Zimmer, *Philosophies of India,* Bollingen Series XXVI (New York, Pantheon Books Inc., 1951), p. 300.

32. *Edda,* "Der Seherin Gesicht," Translated by Felix Genzmer (Düsseldorf/Köln, Eugen Diederichs Verlag, 1956), p. 43.

33. E. T. C. Werner, *Myths and Legends of China* (London: S. Harrap & Co., Ltd., 1922), p. 129.

34. *Ibid,* p. 79.

35. *Edda, op. cit.,* "Das Wafthrudnir Lied," p. 86.

36. *Original Sanskrit Texts,* translated by J. Muir (London, Trübner & Co., 1872), Vol. V, "Rg Veda," X, 129, p. 247.
37. Arthur Llewellyn Basham, *The Wonder that was India* (New York, The Macmillan Company, 1955), p. 238.
38. "The Hymn of Creation," translated by A. L. Basham, *op. cit.,* pp. 247–248.
39. All quotations from the Old and New Testaments are from the standard King James version.
40. L. Ginzberg, *op. cit.,* Vol. I, p. 70.
41. *Ibid,* p. 110.
42. Sophocles I, *Oedipus at Colonos,* translated by Robert Fitzgerald, in *The Complete Greek Tragedies* (Chicago, The University of Chicago Press, 1954), p. 91.
43. L. Ginzberg, *op. cit.,* Vol. V, p. 55.
44. *Ibid,* Vol. I, p. 168.
45. Sigmund Freud, *Collected Papers,* The International Psycho-Analytical Library, Vol. 37 (London, The Hogarth Press, 1950), Vol. V, p. 96.
46. L. Ginzberg, *op. cit.,* Vol. V, p. 243.
47. Origen, *Homilia* V, "In Genesim," pp. 190–194.
48. *Sancti Ephraem Syri In Genesim et in Exodum Commentarium,* ed. R. M. Tonneau, Corpus Scriptorum Christianorum Orientalium Editum Consilio Universitatis Catholicae Americas et Universitatis Catholicae Lovaniensis, Vol. 152, Scriptores Syri, Tomus 71 (Louvain, L. Durbecq, 1955).
49. L. Ginzberg, *op. cit.,* Vol. V, p. 243.
50. Origen, "In Genesim," 32–B. 4, in Migne, *Patres Graeci,* Vol. XII. The second volume of the complete works of Origen, ed. DD. Carolies et Carolies Vin Contius Delarue, 1862.
51. E. Wellisch, *Isaac and Oedipus* (London, Routledge & Kegan Paul, 1954), p. 87.
52. Aeschylus, *Agamemnon,* as translated by Edith Hamilton in *Mythology* (Boston, Little, Brown & Co., 1946), pp. 261–262.
53. Aeschylus, *The Eumenides,* David Grene & Richmond Lattimore, editors, *The Complete Greek Tragedies* (Chicago, The University of Chicago Press, 1957), lines 657–667 and 734–741.
54. Sophocles, *Oedipus at Colonos,* translated by Lewis Campbell. In Gilbert Murray, ed., *Fifteen Greek Plays* (New York, Oxford University Press, 1943), p. 298.
55. T. S. Eliot, "Four Quartets," *The Complete Poems and Plays, 1909–1950* (New York, Harcourt, Brace and Co., 1950), pp. 126–127.
56. L. Ginzberg, *op. cit.,* Vol. I, p. 280.
57. *Ibid,* p. 282.
58. *Ibid,* p. 283.
59. Micha Josef bin Gorion, *op. cit.,* "Die Erzvaeter," p. 295.
60. L. Ginzberg, *op. cit.,* p. 278.

61. *Ibid,* p. 285.
62. Deuteronomy 6:5. Apropos of this passage, we find in Rashi's *Kommentar zum Pentateuch* the following: "With all your heart—*with both your impulses.*"
63. S. Kierkegaard, *Fear and Trembling,* Problem I (Garden City, N. Y., Doubleday Anchor Books, 1955), p. 64.
64. "The connexion of St. George with a dragon, familiar since the *Golden Legend* of Jacobus de Voragine, can be traced to the close of the 6th Century. At Arsuf or Joppa—neither of them far from Lydda—Perseus had slain the sea-monster that threatened the virgin Andromeda, and George, like many another Christian saint, entered into the inheritance of veneration previously enjoyed by a pagan hero. The exploit thus attaches itself to the very common Aryan myth of the sun-god as the conqueror of the powers of darkness." *Encyclopedia Britannica,* Vol. 11, p. 736b–737a, 11th Edition.

    "Mahommedans who usually identify St. George with the prophet Elijah, . . . at Lydda confound his legend with one about Christ himself. Their name for Antichrist is Dajjâl, and they have a tradition that Jesus will slay Antichrist by the gate of Lydda. This notion sprang from a bas-relief of St. George and the Dragon on the Lydda church. But Dajjâl may be derived, by a common confusion between *n* and *l,* from Dagôn, whose name two neighbouring villages bear to this day, while one of the gates of Lydda used to be called the Gate of Dagôn. . . . It is indeed a curious process by which the monster symbolic of heathenism conquered by Christianity has been evolved out of the first great rival of the God of Israel." G. A. Smith, *Historical Geography of the Holy Land* (New York, Ray Long & Richard R. Smith, Inc., 1932), pp. 161–162.
65. L. Ginzberg, *op. cit.,* Vol. V, p. 218.
66. Eusebius, *Chronicon,* A. Schoene, ed. (Berlin, 1875), Vol. I, p. 75.
67. *The Poetic Edda,* "Howamol," translated by Henry Adams Bellows (New York, The American Scandinavian Foundation, 1923), p. 60.
68. L. Ginzberg, *op. cit.,* Vol. I, p. 281.
69. *Ibid,* p. 284.
70. Micha Josef bin Gorion, *op. cit.,* "Die Zwölf Staemme," p. 268.
71. *Ibid,* "Die Erzvaeter," p. 355.
72. L. Ginzberg, *op. cit.,* Vol. I, p. 315.
73. Micha Josef bin Gorion, *op. cit.,* p. 356.
74. Jacob Boehme, *Mysterium Magnum; or An Exposition of the 1st Book of Moses, called Genesis,* translated by John Sparrow, edited by J. C. Barker (London, John M. Watkins Co., 1924), Vol. II, p. 590.
75. The sociological correlative of this incident is primogeniture.
76. L. Ginzberg, *op. cit.,* p. 333.
77. Micha Josef bin Gorion, *op. cit.,* p. 383.
78. *Ibid,* p. 414.

79. L Ginzberg, *op. cit.*, p. 352.
80. *Ibid*, p. 350.
81. Micha Josef bin Gorion, *op. cit.*, "Die Zwölf Staemme," p. 263.
82. Meister Eckhart, *Schriften* (Jena, Eugen Diederichs Verlag, 1934), p. 109.
83. L. Ginzberg, *op. cit.*, p. 354.
84. *Ibid*.
85. *Ibid*, p. 361. Also *Midrash Rabbah*, *op. cit.*, "Genesis, II," LXX, verse 19, p. 650.
86. *The Zohar*, translated by H. Sperling (London, The Soncino Press, 1932), Vol. II, Fol. 144b, p. 65.
87. *Midrash Rabbah*, *op. cit.*, p. 897.
88. Rashi, *Deuteronomie*, 29, 12.

PART THREE

89. Jacques Combes, *Jerome Bosch* (New York, Universal Books, Inc., 1957), pp. 8–9.
90. A. Heidel, *op. cit.*, p. 18.
91. C. G. Jung and Kerenyi, *Einführung in das Wesen der Mythologie* (Zurich, Rascher et Cie., 1941), p. 135.
92. "Rosarium," 1550. As quoted in C. G. Jung, *The Practice of Psychotherapy*, *op. cit.*, pp. 307–308.
93. Sir Herbert Read, from an article in *Quadrum* (L'Association pour la diffusion artistique et culturelle, Brussels, May, 1956), Vol. I, p. 20.
94. T. S. Eliot, *op. cit.*, "Burnt Norton," p. 121.
95. *The Epic of Gilgamish*, translated by R. Campbell Thompson (London, Luzac & Co., 1928), pp. 55–56.
96. Wilhelm Molsdorf, *Christliche Symbolik der Mittelalterlichen Kunst*, 2nd ed. (Leipzig, Karl L. Hiersemann, 1926), p. 67.
97. Sir Herbert Read, from an essay in *Question, A Journal* (London, Hammond & Hammond), Vol. V, No. 1 (1952), p. 54.
98. C. G. Jung, *Das Geheimnis der goldenen Blüte* (Munich, Dorn Verlag, 1929), p. 23ff.
99. Jan Ehrenwald, "Doctrinal Compliance in Psychotherapy," *Progress in Psychotherapy*, Vol. III, p. 44ff.